JESSIE ANTHONY

Job interview Questions SIMPLIFIED

Win Your Dream Job in 30 Days with Insider Secrets and AI-Proof Strategies

Copyright © 2024 by Jessie Anthony

All rights reserved. No part of this publication may be reproduced, stored or transmitted in any form or by any means, electronic, mechanical, photocopying, recording, scanning, or otherwise without written permission from the publisher. It is illegal to copy this book, post it to a website, or distribute it by any other means without permission.

First edition

This book was professionally typeset on Reedsy.
Find out more at reedsy.com

Contents

Introduction: Mastering the Art of Job Interviews in a...	1
Chapter 1: The Modern Job Interview Landscape	6
Chapter 2: Mastering Your Mindset: Confidence and Positivity	12
Chapter 3: Research Techniques: Know Your Potential Employer...	18
Chapter 4: Crafting Your Personal Brand	25
Chapter 5: Resume Optimization for Automatic Tracking...	32
Chapter 6: Understanding the Elevator Pitch	39
Chapter 7: Body Language Secrets: Nonverbal Communication...	46
Chapter 8: Answering Common Questions with the STAR Method	54
Chapter 9: Tackling Behavioral Questions Like a Pro	60
Chapter 10: Navigating Tricky Situational Questions	67
Chapter 11: Showcasing Your Soft Skills Effectively	74
Chapter 12: Technical Interview Strategies (for relevant...	81
Chapter 13: Remote Interview Success: Mastering Virtual...	88
Chapter 14: Group Interview Dynamics: Standing Out in a...	96
Chapter 15: Negotiation Techniques: Salary and Benefits	103
Chapter 16: Following Up: The Often Overlooked Step	110
Chapter 17: Dealing with Rejection and Learning from...	117
Chapter 18: Industry-Specific Interview Tips (customize...	125
Chapter 19: The Future of Interviews: AI and Automation	135
Chapter 20: Your 30-Day Interview Preparation Plan	143
Conclusion: Mastering the Art of Job Interviews	150
Chapter 23	155

Introduction: Mastering the Art of Job Interviews in a Rapidly Changing World

Welcome to "Job Interview Questions SIMPLIFIED: Win Your Dream Job in 30 Days with Insider Secrets and AI-Proof Strategies". If you're holding this book, you're likely at a crucial juncture in your career. Perhaps you're fresh out of college, eager to land your first real job. Maybe you're a seasoned professional looking to make a significant career change. Or you could be somewhere in between, aiming to climb the next rung on your career ladder. Regardless of where you are in your professional journey, one thing is certain: mastering the art of job interviews is essential to your success.

In today's rapidly evolving job market, the interview process has become more complex and nuanced than ever before. Gone are the days when a firm handshake and a well-pressed suit were enough to make a lasting impression. The modern job interview is a multi-faceted challenge that requires preparation, strategy, and adaptability.

Consider this: according to recent studies, the average corporate job opening attracts 250 resumes. Of those candidates, only 4 to 6 will be called for an interview, and only one will be offered the job. These statistics might seem daunting, but they underscore a crucial point: in a sea of qualified candidates, your interview performance can be the decisive factor that sets you apart from the competition.

But here's the good news: interviewing is a skill, and like any skill, it can be learned, honed, and mastered. This book is your comprehensive guide to doing just that.

Why This Book?

You might be wondering, "With thousands of job interview books out there, what makes this one different?" The answer lies in our approach. We've distilled years of research, countless interviews with hiring managers and successful job seekers, and the latest insights from the fields of psychology and neuroscience into a straightforward, actionable 30-day plan.

This isn't just another book filled with generic advice and overused interview questions. Instead, "Job Interview SIMPLIFIED" offers a holistic approach to interview preparation that addresses every aspect of the modern hiring process. From crafting an AI-optimized resume to mastering the nuances of virtual interviews, from understanding the psychology behind behavioral questions to negotiating your salary with confidence, we've got you covered.

The Changing Landscape of Job Interviews

The job market of today bears little resemblance to that of even a decade ago. Technological advancements, shifting work cultures, and global events like the COVID-19 pandemic have dramatically altered the way companies hire. Here are just a few of the changes you need to be prepared for:

1. **The Rise of AI in Hiring**: Many companies now use Artificial Intelligence to screen resumes and even conduct initial interviews. Understanding how these systems work can give you a significant advantage.
2. **Virtual Interviews**: Remote work has made virtual interviews commonplace. Mastering the nuances of video communication is now as important as your in-person interview skills.
3. **Emphasis on Soft Skills**: With technical skills becoming increasingly automated, employers are placing greater emphasis on soft skills like

adaptability, emotional intelligence, and creativity.
4. **Diversity and Inclusion**: Companies are more focused than ever on building diverse teams. Understanding how to communicate your unique perspective and experiences is crucial.
5. **The Gig Economy**: With more people opting for freelance and contract work, interviewing for short-term positions requires a different approach than traditional full-time roles.

What You'll Learn

Over the course of 20 carefully crafted chapters, we'll take you on a journey of self-discovery and skill development. You'll learn:

- How to craft a personal brand that resonates with potential employers
- Techniques to research companies effectively and ask insightful questions
- Strategies to answer even the toughest behavioral and situational questions
- The secrets of body language and nonverbal communication
- How to navigate group interviews and assessment centers
- Techniques for effective salary negotiation
- Strategies for following up after the interview to maximize your chances of success

But this book offers more than just techniques and strategies. It's designed to transform your entire approach to job interviews. By the time you finish, you'll not only be prepared to ace your next interview, but you'll actually look forward to the opportunity to showcase your skills and personality.

The 30-Day Challenge

One of the unique features of this book is our 30-Day Interview Preparation Plan. We understand that looking for a job can be overwhelming, especially when you're trying to balance it with your current work or personal responsibilities. That's why we've broken down the interview preparation process into manageable daily tasks.

Each day, you'll focus on a specific aspect of interview preparation, building your skills and confidence step by step. By the end of the 30 days, you'll have:

- Optimized your resume for both human and AI readers
- Crafted compelling answers to the most common interview questions
- Developed a strong personal brand and elevator pitch
- Mastered the art of virtual interviewing
- Built a network of professional contacts
- And much more

Remember, consistency is key. Commit to following this plan, and you'll see remarkable progress in your interview skills and overall confidence.

A Word on Mindset

Before we dive into the specifics of interview techniques, it's crucial to address the most important factor in your success: your mindset. The job search process can be stressful and, at times, disheartening. You may face rejection or silence from potential employers. But it's essential to maintain a positive, growth-oriented mindset throughout the process.

View each interview, regardless of the outcome, as an opportunity to learn and improve. Embrace the challenges as chances to develop your resilience and adaptability – qualities that are highly valued in today's workplace. Remember, even the most successful professionals have faced rejection at some point in their careers. What sets them apart is their ability to learn from these experiences and keep moving forward.

Your Journey Begins Now

As you embark on this journey to master the art of job interviews, remember that you're not alone. Thousands of people just like you have used the techniques in this book to land their dream jobs, advance their careers, and achieve professional fulfillment.

Whether you're aiming for an entry-level position or a seat in the C-suite, the principles and strategies in this book will give you the edge you need to succeed. So take a deep breath, turn the page, and let's begin your transformation into a confident, skilled interviewee who's ready to win their dream job.

Your future starts now. Let's make it extraordinary.

Chapter 1: The Modern Job Interview Landscape

The job interview process has undergone a dramatic transformation in recent years. Gone are the days when a candidate could simply walk into an office, charm the interviewer with a firm handshake, and land the job based on a pleasant conversation. Today's job interview landscape is a complex, multi-faceted environment that demands a high level of preparation, adaptability, and strategic thinking from candidates. In this chapter, we'll explore the key factors shaping the modern job interview process and how you can navigate this new terrain successfully.

The Digital Revolution

One of the most significant changes in the job interview landscape has been brought about by the digital revolution. Technology has permeated every aspect of the hiring process, from how companies advertise positions to how they conduct interviews.

Online Job Platforms and Application Processes

The first touchpoint for many job seekers is now digital. Online job platforms like LinkedIn, Indeed, and Glassdoor have become the primary marketplaces for job opportunities. These platforms not only list job openings but also allow candidates to apply directly through their interfaces. This shift has several implications:

1. **Volume of Applications**: Companies now receive hundreds, sometimes thousands, of applications for a single position. This means your application needs to stand out from the very beginning.
2. **Applicant Tracking Systems (ATS)**: To manage the high volume of applications, many companies use ATS software to screen resumes before they ever reach human eyes. Understanding how these systems work is crucial for getting your application past the first hurdle.
3. **Digital First Impressions**: Your online presence, including your LinkedIn profile and any other professional social media accounts, has become an extension of your resume. Recruiters often check these profiles before inviting candidates for interviews.

Video Interviews and Virtual Assessments

The COVID-19 pandemic accelerated the adoption of remote work and, consequently, remote hiring processes. Even as in-person work returns in many sectors, video interviews have remained a popular option for initial screening rounds. This shift brings new challenges:

1. **Technical Proficiency**: Candidates need to be comfortable with video conferencing software and troubleshoot basic technical issues.
2. **Virtual Presence**: Presenting yourself professionally on camera requires different skills than in-person interactions. Factors like lighting, background, and camera angle become important considerations.
3. **Digital Body Language**: Reading and projecting non-verbal cues becomes more challenging in a virtual setting, requiring heightened awareness and practice.

AI and Automation in Hiring

Artificial Intelligence is playing an increasingly significant role in the hiring process, influencing everything from resume screening to final selection decisions.

AI-Powered Resume Screening

Many companies now use AI algorithms to scan resumes for relevant keywords, experiences, and qualifications. This means that optimizing your resume for both human and AI readers is crucial.

Automated Initial Interviews

Some companies are using chatbots or AI-driven video interview platforms for initial screening rounds. These systems may ask candidates to answer predetermined questions, with AI analyzing factors like word choice, facial expressions, and tone of voice.

Predictive Analytics

Advanced AI systems are being used to predict a candidate's potential job performance based on their application materials, interview responses, and sometimes even their digital footprint. While the ethics of such practices are debated, it's important to be aware that your online presence may be scrutinized more thoroughly than ever before.

Emphasis on Soft Skills and Cultural Fit

While technical skills remain important, there's been a notable shift towards emphasizing soft skills and cultural fit in the interview process.

CHAPTER 1: THE MODERN JOB INTERVIEW LANDSCAPE

Behavioral Interviews

Many companies now rely heavily on behavioral interview questions, which ask candidates to provide specific examples of how they've handled situations in the past. The theory is that past behavior is the best predictor of future performance.

Situational Judgment Tests

These assessments present candidates with hypothetical work scenarios and ask how they would respond. They're designed to evaluate problem-solving skills, interpersonal abilities, and alignment with company values.

Team Interviews and Culture Panels

More companies are involving multiple team members in the interview process, sometimes conducting panel interviews or culture fit assessments. This approach aims to evaluate how well a candidate would integrate with the existing team and company culture.

Diversity, Equity, and Inclusion (DEI) Initiatives

There's been a growing focus on building diverse and inclusive workplaces, which has influenced the interview process in several ways:

1. **Blind Recruitment**: Some companies use techniques to anonymize applications in the initial stages, removing information like names or photos that could lead to unconscious bias.
2. **Structured Interviews**: To ensure fairness, many organizations are moving towards more structured interview processes where all candidates are asked the same questions in the same order.
3. **Diverse Interview Panels**: Companies are making efforts to ensure that interview panels represent diverse perspectives and backgrounds.

4. **Inclusive Language**: There's increased attention to using inclusive language in job descriptions and throughout the interview process.

The Rise of Project-Based Assessments

Many companies are moving beyond traditional interviews to incorporate project-based assessments. These might include:

1. **Take-Home Assignments**: Candidates might be asked to complete a relevant task or project as part of the application process.
2. **Live Problem-Solving**: Some interviews include real-time problem-solving exercises where candidates work through a challenge related to the role.
3. **Presentations**: Candidates may be asked to prepare and deliver a presentation on a given topic.

These assessments aim to give a more accurate picture of a candidate's skills and how they approach real-world problems.

The Gig Economy and Non-Traditional Roles

The rise of the gig economy and increase in contract, freelance, and remote work opportunities have changed the nature of many job interviews. Candidates may need to demonstrate:

1. **Self-Management Skills**: The ability to work independently and manage one's time effectively.
2. **Adaptability**: Flexibility to work with different teams or on various projects.
3. **Remote Collaboration**: Skills in using digital tools for communication and project management.

Continuous Assessment

The idea that the interview process ends when you get the job is outdated. Many companies now view the first few months of employment as an extended interview period:

1. **Probationary Periods**: These are becoming more common, with formal evaluations at the end.
2. **Onboarding Goals**: New hires may be given specific goals to achieve within their first 30, 60, or 90 days.
3. **Cultural Integration**: How well an employee integrates into the company culture is often closely observed during the initial period of employment.

Conclusion

The modern job interview landscape is complex and ever-evolving. Success in this environment requires a multi-faceted approach: technical preparation, emotional intelligence, adaptability, and a strong personal brand. As we progress through this book, we'll delve deeper into strategies for navigating each of these aspects, equipping you with the tools you need to excel in any interview situation. Remember, while the landscape may seem challenging, it also presents opportunities. By understanding these trends and preparing accordingly, you can position yourself as a standout candidate in any hiring process.

Chapter 2: Mastering Your Mindset: Confidence and Positivity

In the journey to securing your dream job, your greatest asset isn't your resume, your experience, or even your skills. It's your mindset. The way you think about yourself and approach the job interview process can make the difference between success and failure. In this chapter, we'll explore how to cultivate a mindset of confidence and positivity that will not only help you ace your interviews but also set you up for long-term career success.

The Power of Mindset

Before we dive into specific strategies, it's crucial to understand why mindset matters so much in the context of job interviews.

The Self-Fulfilling Prophecy

Psychologists have long recognized the phenomenon of the self-fulfilling prophecy – the idea that our beliefs about ourselves and our capabilities can actually influence our outcomes. If you believe you're going to fail an interview, you're more likely to behave in ways that lead to failure. Conversely, if you believe in your ability to succeed, you're more likely to take actions that lead to success.

CHAPTER 2: MASTERING YOUR MINDSET: CONFIDENCE AND POSITIVITY

The Confidence-Competence Loop

Confidence and competence are intimately linked. As you become more competent, you naturally become more confident. But interestingly, the reverse is also true. When you project confidence, you're more likely to take on challenges that increase your competence. This creates a positive feedback loop that can propel your career forward.

The Impact on Others

Your mindset doesn't just affect you; it affects how others perceive you. Interviewers are more likely to respond positively to candidates who exude confidence and positivity. These qualities signal that you're capable, resilient, and pleasant to work with – all highly desirable traits in any employee.

Building Unshakeable Confidence

Confidence isn't something you're born with; it's a skill you can develop. Here are some strategies to build your confidence:

1. Prepare Thoroughly

Nothing builds confidence like being well-prepared. This means not just researching the company and practicing common interview questions, but also deeply understanding your own value proposition. What unique combination of skills, experiences, and perspectives do you bring to the table? The more clearly you can articulate this, the more confident you'll feel.

2. Visualize Success

Athletes have long used visualization techniques to improve performance, and you can too. Spend time each day visualizing yourself succeeding in your interview. Imagine yourself answering questions with ease, building rapport with the interviewer, and leaving the interview feeling triumphant. This mental rehearsal can significantly boost your confidence when it's time for the real thing.

3. Practice Power Posing

Amy Cuddy's famous TED talk introduced the world to the concept of power posing – the idea that our body language can influence our mental state. Before your interview, take a few minutes to stand in a "power pose" (think Wonder Woman stance). This can actually increase your testosterone levels and decrease cortisol, leaving you feeling more confident and less stressed.

4. Reframe Negative Self-Talk

We all have an inner critic, but letting it run wild can be detrimental to your confidence. Learn to catch negative self-talk and reframe it positively. Instead of "I'm not qualified for this job," try "This is a great opportunity for me to grow and learn." Instead of "I always mess up interviews," try "Each interview is a chance for me to improve my skills."

5. Celebrate Past Successes

Take time to reflect on your past achievements, no matter how small. Keep a "success journal" where you record your accomplishments. Review this before interviews to remind yourself of your capabilities and boost your confidence.

CHAPTER 2: MASTERING YOUR MINDSET: CONFIDENCE AND POSITIVITY

Cultivating Positivity

While confidence is crucial, maintaining a positive outlook is equally important. Here's how to foster positivity:

1. Practice Gratitude

Regularly acknowledging the good things in your life, even during a challenging job search, can significantly boost your mood and outlook. Each day, write down three things you're grateful for. This simple practice can shift your focus from what's lacking to what's abundant in your life.

2. Surround Yourself with Positivity

The people and information you surround yourself with can greatly influence your mindset. Seek out positive, supportive friends and mentors. Consume uplifting content, whether it's books, podcasts, or social media accounts focused on personal development and career success.

3. Embrace a Growth Mindset

Developed by psychologist Carol Dweck, the concept of a growth mindset is the belief that your abilities can be developed through dedication and hard work. Embrace challenges as opportunities to grow, view effort as the path to mastery, and see failures as valuable learning experiences.

4. Practice Self-Care

It's hard to maintain a positive outlook if you're burned out or neglecting your physical and mental health. Make sure you're getting enough sleep, eating well, exercising regularly, and taking time for activities you enjoy. A healthy body and mind are the foundation of a positive outlook.

5. Find the Lesson in Every Experience

Even if an interview doesn't result in a job offer, there's always something to be learned. Maybe you discovered a new industry you're interested in, or you realized you need to brush up on certain skills. By focusing on the lessons and growth opportunities in every experience, you can maintain a positive outlook even in the face of setbacks.

Handling Interview Anxiety

Even with all these strategies, it's normal to feel some anxiety about job interviews. Here are some techniques to manage those nerves:

1. Breathe

Simple breathing exercises can do wonders for calming your nerves. Try the 4-7-8 technique: inhale for 4 counts, hold for 7 counts, and exhale for 8 counts. Repeat this a few times before your interview to center yourself.

2. Reframe Anxiety as Excitement

Anxiety and excitement are physiologically similar emotions. By consciously reframing your anxiety as excitement ("I'm not nervous, I'm excited about this opportunity!"), you can shift your mindset from threat to challenge.

3. Focus on Service

Instead of obsessing over your performance, focus on how you can be of service to the company. How can your skills and experiences help solve their problems? This shift in focus can alleviate self-conscious anxiety and help you connect more authentically with the interviewer.

4. Use Positive Affirmations

Develop a set of positive affirmations that resonate with you. These might include statements like "I am well-prepared and qualified for this position" or "I bring unique value to every team I'm part of." Repeat these to yourself before and during the interview process.

The Long Game: Building Resilience

Remember, mastering your mindset isn't just about nailing a single interview; it's about building long-term resilience in your career. The job search process can be challenging, and even the most qualified candidates face rejection sometimes. By cultivating confidence and positivity, you're equipping yourself to bounce back from setbacks, learn from every experience, and continually move forward in your career journey.

As you work through the strategies in this chapter, be patient with yourself. Changing your mindset is a process, not an overnight transformation. Celebrate small victories, be kind to yourself when you struggle, and keep pushing forward. With time and practice, you'll develop the unshakeable confidence and positive outlook that will not only help you ace your interviews but thrive in every aspect of your career.

Remember, the most successful professionals aren't necessarily the most skilled or experienced – they're the ones who believe in themselves, maintain a positive outlook in the face of challenges, and never stop growing. By mastering your mindset, you're setting yourself up for success not just in your next interview, but in your entire career journey.

Chapter 3: Research Techniques: Know Your Potential Employer Inside Out

In the competitive landscape of job hunting, thorough research about your potential employer can be the key differentiator that sets you apart from other candidates. It's not just about impressing the interviewer with your knowledge; it's about determining if the company is the right fit for you and preparing yourself to ask insightful questions. In this chapter, we'll explore effective techniques to research your potential employer and how to use this information to your advantage during the interview process.

Why Research Matters

Before we dive into the techniques, let's understand why this research is so crucial:

1. **Demonstrates Interest and Initiative**: Thorough research shows the employer that you're genuinely interested in the position and the company.
2. **Helps You Tailor Your Responses**: Understanding the company's values, challenges, and goals allows you to frame your answers in a way that resonates with their needs.
3. **Builds Confidence**: The more you know about the company, the more confident you'll feel during the interview.
4. **Aids in Decision Making**: Your research will help you determine if

the company culture and values align with your own.
5. **Prepares You for Questions**: Many interviewers will ask what you know about their company. Your research prepares you for this.

Research Techniques

Now, let's explore various techniques you can use to gather comprehensive information about your potential employer.

1. Company Website Deep Dive

Start with the company's official website. Don't just skim the surface; dive deep into every section.

- **About Us Page**: This often contains the company's history, mission statement, and values.
- **Products/Services**: Understand what the company offers in detail.
- **News/Press Releases**: These provide insight into recent developments and future directions.
- **Careers Page**: This can give you an idea of the company culture and values they prioritize in employees.
- **Leadership Team**: Familiarize yourself with key executives and their backgrounds.

2. Social Media Analysis

A company's social media presence can provide valuable insights into its culture, communication style, and current focus areas.

- **LinkedIn**: Look at the company page, but also check out profiles of current employees to understand their backgrounds and roles.
- **Twitter**: Often used for real-time updates and engagement with customers.

- **Facebook/Instagram**: These platforms might showcase the company culture and behind-the-scenes glimpses.
- **YouTube**: Many companies have channels with product demos, employee interviews, or corporate events.

3. Financial Reports and Earnings Calls

For publicly traded companies, these are goldmines of information.

- **Annual Reports**: These provide a comprehensive overview of the company's financial health and strategic direction.
- **Quarterly Earnings Calls**: Listen to or read transcripts of these calls to understand current challenges and priorities.
- **SEC Filings**: These can provide detailed information about the company's operations, risks, and financial status.

4. Industry News and Analysis

Understanding the broader context of the industry can provide valuable talking points.

- **Industry-Specific Publications**: Subscribe to or regularly check relevant trade journals or websites.
- **General Business News**: Publications like Forbes, Bloomberg, or The Wall Street Journal often provide industry analysis.
- **Competitor Analysis**: Research the company's main competitors to understand its market position.

5. Employee Reviews and Insights

While these should be taken with a grain of salt, they can provide valuable insider perspectives.

- **Glassdoor:** Read employee reviews, but look for patterns rather than focusing on individual comments.
- **Indeed**: Another source of employee reviews and salary information.
- **LinkedIn**: Look for posts or articles from current or former employees.

6. Networking and Informational Interviews

If possible, connect with current or former employees for insider insights.

- **LinkedIn Connections**: See if you have any connections who work or have worked at the company.
- **Alumni Networks**: Your school's alumni network might include employees of the company.
- **Professional Associations**: Industry events can be great opportunities to meet company representatives.

7. Company Products or Services

If possible, become a user of the company's products or services.

- **Try the Product**: If it's a consumer product, try it out yourself.
- **Customer Reviews**: Read what customers are saying about the product or service.
- **App Store/Play Store**: For tech companies, read reviews of their apps.

Organizing Your Research

As you gather information, it's crucial to organize it effectively. Here's a suggested structure:

1. **Company Overview**: Brief history, mission statement, core values.
2. **Products/Services**: Key offerings and their market position.
3. **Recent News**: Major developments in the last 6-12 months.

4. **Financial Health**: Key financial metrics and trends (for public companies).
5. **Culture and Work Environment**: Insights from employee reviews and company communications.
6. **Industry Position**: Main competitors and the company's unique selling points.
7. **Challenges and Opportunities**: Both company-specific and industry-wide.
8. **Your Fit**: How your skills and experiences align with the company's needs and values.

Using Your Research in the Interview

Now that you've done your research, how do you use it effectively in the interview?

1. Tailor Your Answers

Use your knowledge of the company to frame your responses to interview questions. For example, if you know the company values innovation, emphasize your creative problem-solving skills with specific examples.

2. Ask Insightful Questions

Your research should enable you to ask thoughtful questions that show your genuine interest and understanding of the company. For example:

- "I noticed in your recent press release that you're expanding into [new market]. How does this align with the company's five-year plan?"
- "Your CEO mentioned in the last earnings call that [specific challenge] is a priority. How is this impacting roles in this department?"

3. Draw Parallels

Connect your experiences with the company's needs or values. For instance, "I see that sustainability is a core value for your company. In my previous role, I led an initiative that reduced our carbon footprint by 20%."

4. Demonstrate Industry Knowledge

Show that you understand not just the company, but its place in the broader industry. This could involve discussing industry trends or comparing the company's approach to that of its competitors.

5. Address Company Challenges

If you've identified specific challenges the company is facing, tactfully bring these up and discuss how your skills could contribute to addressing them.

Balancing Act: Don't Overdo It

While thorough research is crucial, be careful not to come across as a know-it-all or to reveal information that might be considered confidential. The goal is to demonstrate informed interest, not to recite the company's entire history.

Continuous Learning

Remember, your research shouldn't stop after the first interview. Continue to stay updated on company news between interviews and before starting the job. This ongoing curiosity will serve you well throughout your career.

Conclusion

Researching your potential employer is more than just a pre-interview task; it's a skill that will serve you throughout your career. By thoroughly understanding the company, its industry, and your potential place within it, you position yourself as a candidate who is not just looking for any job, but for the right opportunity to contribute and grow. This level of preparation demonstrates your professionalism, genuine interest, and strategic thinking – qualities that are highly valued by employers across all industries.

Remember, the goal of your research is not just to impress the interviewer, but to help you make an informed decision about your career. The insights you gain will help you determine if the company is the right fit for your skills, values, and career aspirations. With thorough research, you enter the interview not just as a candidate, but as a well-informed potential colleague ready to contribute from day one.

Chapter 4: Crafting Your Personal Brand

In today's competitive job market, having the right skills and experience is crucial, but it's often not enough to stand out from the crowd. To truly differentiate yourself, you need to develop a strong personal brand. Your personal brand is the unique combination of skills, experiences, and personality that you want the world to see. It's the story you tell about yourself, the values you stand for, and the impression you leave on others. In this chapter, we'll explore how to craft a compelling personal brand that will make you memorable to potential employers and set you up for long-term career success.

Understanding Personal Branding

Before we dive into the how-to, let's clarify what we mean by personal branding:

What is a Personal Brand?

Your personal brand is the professional image you project to the world. It's how you market yourself to potential employers, colleagues, and clients. It encompasses your skills, your values, your unique experiences, and the way you communicate all of these elements.

Why is Personal Branding Important?

1. **Differentiation**: In a sea of qualified candidates, a strong personal brand helps you stand out.
2. **Consistency**: It provides a consistent narrative across all professional interactions and platforms.
3. **Authenticity**: It allows you to present your genuine self, attracting opportunities that align with your values and goals.
4. **Career Advancement**: A well-crafted personal brand can open doors to new opportunities and accelerate your career growth.
5. **Trust and Credibility**: A strong personal brand builds trust with employers, colleagues, and clients.

Steps to Craft Your Personal Brand

Now, let's explore the process of developing your personal brand:

1. Self-Reflection and Assessment

The first step in crafting your personal brand is to understand yourself deeply.

- **Identify Your Strengths**: What are you exceptionally good at? What skills or qualities do others often compliment you on?
- **Clarify Your Values**: What principles guide your decisions and actions?
- **Define Your Passions**: What work excites you? What causes do you care deeply about?
- **Assess Your Unique Experiences**: What life or work experiences set you apart?

Try this exercise: Write down 10 adjectives that describe you professionally. Then, ask colleagues or mentors to do the same for you. Compare the lists to gain insight into how you see yourself versus how others perceive you.

2. Determine Your Target Audience

Your personal brand should be tailored to resonate with your intended audience.

- **Identify Ideal Employers**: Research the values and culture of companies you aspire to work for.
- **Understand Industry Trends**: What skills and qualities are most valued in your field?
- **Consider Career Goals**: How does your personal brand align with your long-term career objectives?

3. Craft Your Personal Brand Statement

Distill your self-reflection into a concise personal brand statement. This should be a one or two-sentence summary of who you are professionally, what you do, and what makes you unique.

For example: "I'm a data scientist who combines analytical rigor with creative problem-solving to uncover insights that drive business growth. My background in both computer science and psychology allows me to bridge the gap between complex algorithms and human behavior."

4. Develop Your Narrative

Expand your brand statement into a compelling narrative. This should include:

- Your professional journey: How did you get to where you are?
- Key achievements: What significant impacts have you made?
- Your unique value proposition: What can you offer that others can't?
- Your vision: Where do you see yourself going in your career?

Remember, storytelling is powerful. Frame your experiences into a narrative that engages and inspires your audience.

5. Visual Branding

Your personal brand isn't just about words; it's also about visual presentation.

- **Professional Photo**: Invest in a high-quality, professional headshot.
- **Consistent Color Scheme**: Choose colors that reflect your personality and use them consistently across platforms.
- **Personal Logo**: Consider creating a simple personal logo for use on your resume, portfolio, or business cards.

6. Online Presence

In the digital age, your online presence is a crucial component of your personal brand.

- **LinkedIn Profile**: Ensure it's complete, professional, and aligned with your brand narrative.
- **Personal Website or Portfolio**: Showcase your work and share your thoughts on industry trends.
- **Social Media**: Curate your posts to reflect your professional brand. Share industry insights, your work, and your thoughts on professional matters.
- **Content Creation**: Consider starting a blog, podcast, or YouTube channel to share your expertise and build your authority in your field.

7. Networking and Relationship Building

Your personal brand is not just what you say about yourself, but also what others say about you.

- **Attend Industry Events**: Engage with peers and thought leaders in

your field.
- **Seek Speaking Opportunities**: Present at conferences or webinars to establish yourself as an expert.
- **Mentor Others**: Helping others not only builds good will but also reinforces your expertise.
- **Seek Testimonials**: Collect and showcase recommendations from colleagues, clients, or managers.

8. Consistency is Key

Ensure your personal brand is consistent across all touchpoints:

- **Resume**: Align your resume's language and presentation with your personal brand.
- **Cover Letter**: Use it as an opportunity to tell your brand story.
- **Interview Responses**: Practice articulating your brand narrative in interview settings.
- **Email Communication**: Your email signature and communication style should reflect your brand.
- **Networking Interactions**: Be consistent in how you present yourself in professional settings.

9. Evolve and Adapt

Your personal brand isn't static; it should evolve as you grow professionally.

- **Regular Self-Assessment**: Periodically revisit your brand to ensure it still aligns with your goals and values.
- **Seek Feedback**: Regularly ask for feedback from trusted colleagues or mentors.
- **Stay Current**: Keep your skills and industry knowledge up-to-date to maintain the relevance of your brand.

Authenticity: The Key to a Sustainable Personal Brand

While crafting your personal brand, it's crucial to remain authentic. Your brand should be an accurate, albeit polished, representation of who you are. Trying to present a false image is not only ethically questionable but also unsustainable in the long run.

- **Be Honest**: Don't exaggerate your skills or experiences.
- **Embrace Your Quirks**: The unique aspects of your personality can be what makes your brand memorable.
- **Admit Mistakes**: Being open about failures and what you've learned from them can strengthen your brand.
- **Show Your Human Side**: While maintaining professionalism, don't be afraid to show your personality and interests outside of work.

Leveraging Your Personal Brand in Job Interviews

Once you've crafted your personal brand, use it to your advantage in job interviews:

1. **Elevator Pitch**: Develop a concise introduction that encapsulates your personal brand.
2. **Brand-Aligned Answers**: Frame your responses to interview questions in a way that reinforces your brand narrative.
3. **Ask Brand-Reinforcing Questions**: The questions you ask can also strengthen your brand image.
4. **Leave-Behind Materials**: Consider creating a branded one-pager or portfolio that summarizes your key strengths and achievements.

Conclusion

Crafting a strong personal brand is an investment in your professional future. It requires self-reflection, strategic thinking, and consistent effort, but the payoff can be significant. A well-developed personal brand can open doors to new opportunities, position you as a leader in your field, and provide a framework for continued professional growth.

Remember, your personal brand is more than just a tool for job hunting; it's a way of intentionally shaping your professional identity and guiding your career trajectory. By clearly communicating who you are, what you stand for, and the unique value you bring, you not only make yourself more attractive to potential employers but also set yourself up for long-term success and fulfillment in your career.

As you move forward in your job search and beyond, let your personal brand be your north star, guiding your decisions and helping you navigate the complex landscape of your professional journey.

Chapter 5: Resume Optimization for Automatic Tracking Systems (ATS)

In today's digital age, before your resume reaches human eyes, it often must first pass through an Applicant Tracking System (ATS). These software systems are used by a majority of medium to large companies to streamline their hiring process, filtering and ranking resumes based on specific criteria. Understanding how ATS works and optimizing your resume accordingly can significantly increase your chances of landing an interview. In this chapter, we'll explore strategies to create an ATS-friendly resume that also impresses human recruiters.

Understanding ATS

Before we dive into optimization techniques, it's crucial to understand what an ATS is and how it works.

What is an ATS?

An Applicant Tracking System is a software application that helps companies manage their recruitment process. It collects, sorts, scans, and ranks the job applications a company receives for their open positions.

How Does an ATS Work?

1. **Parsing**: The ATS breaks down your resume into categories (e.g., work experience, education, skills).
2. **Keyword Matching**: It searches for specific keywords related to the job description.
3. **Ranking**: Resumes are scored based on how well they match the job requirements.
4. **Filtering**: Low-scoring resumes may be automatically rejected.

Key Strategies for ATS Optimization

Now that we understand the basics of ATS, let's explore how to optimize your resume to pass through these systems successfully.

1. Use the Right File Format

- **Stick to Simple Formats**: Use .docx or .pdf files. Avoid .pages, .odt, or other less common formats.
- **Choose ATS-Friendly PDFs**: If using PDF, ensure it's a text-based PDF, not a scanned image.

2. Keep the Layout Simple

- **Avoid Complex Formatting**: Tables, columns, headers, footers, and text boxes can confuse ATS.
- **Use Standard Section Headings**: "Work Experience," "Education," "Skills," etc.
- **Stick to Standard Fonts**: Arial, Calibri, or Times New Roman in 10-12 point size.
- **Use Simple Bullet Points**: Stick to standard circular bullets.

3. Optimize for Keywords

- **Analyze the Job Description**: Identify key skills, qualifications, and experiences mentioned.
- **Include Relevant Keywords**: Naturally incorporate these keywords into your resume.
- **Use Variations**: Include both spelled-out terms and acronyms (e.g., "Search Engine Optimization (SEO)").
- **Create a Skills Section**: List key hard skills relevant to the job.

4. Tailor Your Resume for Each Application

- **Customize for Each Job**: Adjust your resume to highlight the most relevant experiences and skills for each position.
- **Mirror the Language**: Use similar phrases and terms as those in the job description.

5. Provide Context for Keywords

- **Don't Just List Keywords**: Provide context and achievements related to each skill or experience.
- **Use Metrics**: Quantify your achievements where possible (e.g., "Increased sales by 30%").

6. Avoid Overoptimization

- **Don't Keyword Stuff**: Excessive use of keywords can flag your resume as spam.
- **Maintain Readability**: Remember, if your resume passes the ATS, a human will read it next.

7. Use Standard Resume Sections

- **Include Essential Sections**: Contact Information, Summary/Objective, Work Experience, Education, Skills.
- **Order Matters**: Place the most relevant sections higher on your resume.

8. Optimize Your Job Titles

- **Use Standard Job Titles**: If your official title is unique, consider including a standard equivalent in parentheses.
- **Avoid Special Characters**: Don't use special characters or abbreviations in job titles.

9. Include Location Information

- **List City and State**: For each job, include the city and state. Some ATS use this for screening.

10. Format Dates Consistently

- **Use a Clear Format**: MM/YYYY or Month YYYY consistently throughout.
- **Include Both Start and End Dates**: For each position, clearly state when you started and ended.

11. Avoid Images and Graphics

- **Text Only**: ATS cannot read information contained in images.
- **No Fancy Design Elements**: Stick to plain text formatting.

12. Use a Reverse Chronological Format

- **List Most Recent First**: This is the preferred format for most ATS.
- **Include All Relevant Experience**: Don't leave out older relevant experiences.

13. Optimize Your File Name

- **Use a Clear, Professional File Name**: E.g., "John_Doe_Resume_Marketing_Manager.pdf"

14. Check Your Contact Information

- **Place at the Top**: Ensure your name and contact information are at the top of the document.
- **One Phone Number**: Include only one phone number to avoid confusion.

15. Use a Simple Summary or Objective Statement

- **Keep it Concise**: A brief, keyword-rich summary can help set the tone for your resume.
- **Tailor it to the Job**: Adjust your summary to match the specific position you're applying for.

Testing Your ATS-Optimized Resume

After optimizing your resume, it's important to test it:

1. **Use ATS Resume Scanners**: There are online tools that simulate ATS and provide feedback.
2. **Compare with Job Description**: Ensure your resume reflects the key requirements listed.

3. **Peer Review**: Have someone in your industry review your resume for relevance and readability.

Balancing ATS Optimization and Human Appeal

While optimizing for ATS is crucial, remember that your resume should still be appealing and readable to human recruiters. Here are some tips to strike this balance:

1. **Maintain a Clean Design**: While keeping it simple, ensure the layout is visually appealing.
2. **Tell Your Story**: Beyond keywords, make sure your resume narrates your professional journey coherently.
3. **Highlight Achievements**: Use strong action verbs and specific accomplishments to engage human readers.
4. **Personalize**: Include a brief personal statement or objective that shows your enthusiasm for the role.
5. **Proofread**: Ensure there are no spelling or grammatical errors, which both ATS and humans will notice.

When ATS May Not Apply

It's worth noting that not all companies use ATS, particularly smaller businesses or for executive-level positions. In these cases:

1. **Research the Company**: Try to find out if they use an ATS.
2. **Follow Application Instructions**: Some companies may prefer a particular format or additional documents.
3. **Consider a Dual Approach**: Prepare both an ATS-optimized version and a more creatively formatted version of your resume.

Conclusion

Optimizing your resume for Applicant Tracking Systems is no longer optional in today's job market – it's a necessity. By understanding how these systems work and tailoring your resume accordingly, you significantly increase your chances of getting past the initial screening and into the hands of a human recruiter.

Remember, the goal is not to game the system, but to present your qualifications clearly and effectively in a format that both ATS and human recruiters can easily understand. Your resume should be a true representation of your skills and experiences, optimized to ensure that these qualifications are recognized and valued.

As you apply these strategies, keep in mind that the job search process is iterative. If you're not getting the results you want, don't be afraid to revisit and refine your resume. Each application is an opportunity to learn and improve.

Lastly, while an ATS-optimized resume is crucial, it's just one part of a successful job search strategy. Networking, tailoring your application to each position, and preparing for interviews are equally important steps in landing your dream job. Use this optimized resume as a strong foundation, and build upon it with enthusiasm, perseverance, and a commitment to showcasing your unique value to potential employers.

Chapter 6: Understanding the Elevator Pitch

What is an Elevator Pitch?

An elevator pitch is a 30-60 second summary of your professional background, skills, and goals. It's designed to quickly convey your value proposition to potential employers, networking contacts, or anyone who asks, "Tell me about yourself."

Why is it Important?

1. **First Impressions**: Often, your elevator pitch is the first substantial information someone learns about you.
2. **Networking**: It's a crucial tool for making connections at industry events, job fairs, or casual encounters.
3. **Interviews**: Many interviews start with "Tell me about yourself," making your elevator pitch the perfect response.
4. **Confidence**: Having a well-prepared pitch boosts your confidence in professional settings.

Crafting Your Elevator Pitch

Creating an effective elevator pitch involves several key steps:

1. Know Your Audience

- **Research**: Understand the interests and needs of your likely audience.
- **Tailor**: Adjust your pitch based on who you're talking to (e.g., a potential employer vs. a networking contact).

2. Start with a Hook

- **Grab Attention**: Begin with an intriguing statement or question.
- **Be Unique**: Avoid clichés and generic openings.

Example: "Have you ever wondered how companies can turn vast amounts of data into actionable insights? That's where I come in."

3. Introduce Yourself

- **Name and Role**: Clearly state your name and current or desired professional role.
- **Passion**: Briefly mention what drives you in your work.

Example: "I'm Sarah Johnson, a data scientist passionate about helping businesses make data-driven decisions."

4. Highlight Your Unique Value Proposition

- **Key Skills**: Mention 2-3 core skills or experiences that set you apart.
- **Achievements**: Briefly touch on a significant accomplishment.

Example: "With my background in statistics and machine learning, I've helped companies increase their revenue by up to 30% through predictive analytics."

5. Explain Your Goals

- **Career Objectives**: Briefly mention what you're looking for in your career.
- **Alignment**: Show how your goals align with the listener's potential needs.

Example: "I'm looking to bring my expertise to a forward-thinking tech company that's leveraging big data to solve real-world problems."

6. End with a Call to Action

- **Next Steps**: Suggest a way to continue the conversation.
- **Be Specific**: Ask for something concrete, like a meeting or a referral.

Example: "I'd love to learn more about the data challenges in your industry. Could we schedule a brief call to discuss further?"

7. Practice, Practice, Practice

- **Memorize Key Points**: Know your main points by heart, but don't sound robotic.
- **Time Yourself**: Ensure your pitch fits within 30-60 seconds.
- **Record Yourself**: Listen to your pitch and refine it.

Delivering Your Elevator Pitch

Crafting your pitch is only half the battle. Delivering it effectively is equally crucial:

1. Be Confident

- **Body Language**: Stand or sit up straight, make eye contact, and smile.
- **Voice**: Speak clearly and at a moderate pace.
- **Energy**: Show enthusiasm for your work and goals.

2. Be Natural

- **Conversational Tone**: Deliver your pitch as if you're having a conversation, not reciting a script.
- **Flexibility**: Be prepared to adjust your pitch based on the listener's reactions or questions.

3. Read the Room

- **Timing**: Ensure it's an appropriate moment to deliver your pitch.
- **Length**: Be prepared to shorten or extend your pitch based on the situation.

4. Listen and Engage

- **Two-Way Conversation**: Allow for interruptions and questions.
- **Show Interest**: Be ready to learn about the other person as well.

5. Follow Up

- **Business Card**: Have your contact information ready to share.
- **LinkedIn**: Suggest connecting on LinkedIn to continue the professional relationship.

Common Pitfalls to Avoid

As you craft and deliver your elevator pitch, be wary of these common mistakes:

1. **Information Overload**: Don't try to cram your entire resume into 60 seconds.
2. **Being Too Vague**: Avoid general statements that could apply to anyone.
3. **Sounding Rehearsed**: While preparation is key, your delivery should feel natural.
4. **Neglecting to Tailor**: Avoid using the exact same pitch for every situation.
5. **Forgetting the Call to Action**: Always end with a clear next step.

Elevator Pitch Templates

While your pitch should be unique to you, here are some templates to get you started:

The Problem Solver

"Hi, I'm [Name]. You know how [describe a common industry problem]? Well, I [explain how you solve that problem]. For example, I recently [share a brief success story]. I'm looking to bring this expertise to [type of company/role you're seeking]. What challenges is your team facing in this area?"

The Career Transition

"Hello, I'm [Name]. After [number] years in [current/previous field], I'm leveraging my experience in [relevant skills] to transition into [new field]. I'm particularly excited about [aspect of new field], and I've been [mention relevant preparation/study]. I'd love to hear about your experience in this industry. Do you have any advice for someone looking to break in?"

The Recent Graduate

"Nice to meet you, I'm [Name]. I recently graduated from [University] with a degree in [Field]. During my studies, I [mention a relevant project or internship]. I'm particularly passionate about [aspect of your field] and I'm seeking opportunities to [what you want to do] in the [industry] sector. What trends are you seeing in entry-level roles in this field?"

Adapting Your Pitch for Different Scenarios

Your elevator pitch should be adaptable to various situations:

1. **Job Fairs**: Focus on your career goals and how they align with companies present.
2. **Networking Events**: Emphasize your current projects and industry insights.
3. **Informational Interviews**: Highlight your curiosity and specific questions about the industry.
4. **Social Settings**: Keep it light and focus on the most interesting aspects of your work.

Conclusion

Mastering the art of the elevator pitch is a crucial skill in today's competitive job market. It's your opportunity to make a strong first impression and open doors to new opportunities. Remember, a great elevator pitch is not about selling yourself aggressively, but about starting a meaningful conversation.

As you craft and refine your pitch, keep in mind that it's a living document. As your career evolves, so should your elevator pitch. Regularly update it to reflect new skills, experiences, and goals.

Lastly, while having a well-prepared elevator pitch is important, the key to its effectiveness lies in your authenticity and passion. Let your genuine enthusiasm for your work shine through, and you'll find that your elevator pitch becomes not just a tool for job hunting, but a powerful asset for building meaningful professional relationships throughout your career.

With practice and refinement, your elevator pitch will become a natural part of your professional persona, ready to be deployed whenever an opportunity arises. So take the time to craft your pitch, practice it regularly, and watch as it opens doors to exciting new possibilities in your career journey.

Chapter 7: Body Language Secrets: Nonverbal Communication Mastery

In the realm of job interviews and professional interactions, what you say is only part of the message you convey. Your body language—the nonverbal cues you send through your posture, gestures, facial expressions, and even your tone of voice—can speak volumes. In fact, studies suggest that nonverbal communication can account for up to 93% of the message you're sending. Mastering the art of body language can give you a significant edge in your job search and career advancement. In this chapter, we'll explore the secrets of effective nonverbal communication and how to use them to your advantage.

Understanding Nonverbal Communication

Nonverbal communication encompasses all the ways we convey messages without words. This includes:

1. Facial Expressions
2. Body Posture
3. Gestures
4. Eye Contact
5. Touch
6. Space
7. Voice (tone, pitch, volume)

Each of these elements plays a crucial role in how we're perceived by others, often on a subconscious level.

The Impact of Body Language in Professional Settings

In a job interview or professional meeting, your body language can:

1. Demonstrate Confidence
2. Show Engagement and Interest
3. Build Rapport and Trust
4. Reinforce Your Verbal Messages
5. Reveal Your Emotional State

Conversely, poor body language can undermine your words, making you appear nervous, disinterested, or even dishonest.

Key Body Language Techniques for Professional Success

1. The Power of a Good Handshake

A handshake is often the first physical contact you'll have with an interviewer or new professional contact.

- Grip: Firm but not crushing
- Duration: 2-3 seconds
- Eye Contact: Maintain throughout the handshake
- Smile: A genuine smile conveys warmth and openness

Practice your handshake with friends or family to ensure you're striking the right balance.

2. Mastering Eye Contact

Effective eye contact is crucial for building trust and showing confidence.

- Maintain eye contact for 50-60% of the time while speaking
- Hold eye contact for 70-80% of the time while listening
- In group settings, make eye contact with each person for a few seconds at a time

Avoid staring, which can make others uncomfortable. Instead, practice the "triangle technique": move your gaze between the person's eyes and mouth in a triangular pattern.

3. Posture Perfect

Your posture can convey confidence, attentiveness, and professionalism.

- Sit or stand up straight with your shoulders back
- Keep your chin parallel to the ground
- Avoid crossing your arms, which can appear defensive
- In a seated position, lean slightly forward to show engagement

Remember the acronym SOFTEN:

- Smile
- Open Posture
- Forward Lean
- Touch (appropriate, like a handshake)
- Eye Contact
- Nod

4. Gestures That Emphasize and Engage

Using hand gestures can make you appear more enthusiastic and can help emphasize key points.

- Use open palm gestures to convey honesty
- Keep gestures within the area between your chest and your waist
- Match the size of your gestures to the size of your points
- Avoid fidgeting or nervous gestures like playing with your hair or jewelry

5. Mirroring and Matching

Subtly mirroring the body language of your interviewer can help build rapport.

- Match their energy level and speaking pace
- Adopt similar postures
- Use similar gestures

Be subtle; obvious mirroring can appear insincere or manipulative.

6. Managing Nervous Habits

We all have nervous habits, but in a professional setting, they can be distracting.

- Identify your nervous habits (e.g., leg shaking, pen clicking)
- Practice awareness of these habits
- Develop replacement behaviors (e.g., pressing your fingertips together instead of fidgeting)

7. The Power of a Smile

A genuine smile can transform the atmosphere of an interaction.

- Smile when you greet someone
- Use a natural smile when discussing topics you're passionate about
- Remember that a genuine smile involves the eyes (known as a Duchenne smile)

8. Mastering Your Voice

While not strictly "body language," your voice is a crucial part of nonverbal communication.

- Speak clearly and at a moderate pace
- Vary your tone to avoid monotony
- Use pauses for emphasis
- Match the volume of your voice to the setting

Reading and Responding to Others' Body Language

Being adept at nonverbal communication isn't just about managing your own body language; it's also about reading and responding to the cues of others.

1. Signs of Engagement

Look for these signs that your interviewer or conversational partner is engaged:

- Leaning forward
- Maintaining eye contact
- Nodding

- Mirroring your posture

2. Signs of Discomfort or Disinterest

Be aware of cues that might indicate discomfort or disinterest:

- Crossed arms
- Leaning away
- Limited eye contact
- Checking the time or phone

If you notice these signs, try changing your approach or the subject of conversation.

3. Recognizing Incongruence

Pay attention when someone's words don't match their body language. This incongruence can reveal true feelings or thoughts.

Body Language in Virtual Settings

With the rise of remote work and video interviews, mastering body language in virtual settings has become crucial.

1. Camera Placement

Position your camera at eye level to simulate natural eye contact.

2. Framing

Frame yourself from the chest up, allowing room for hand gestures.

3. Background

Ensure your background is professional and not distracting.

4. Lighting

Use good lighting that illuminates your face clearly.

5. Eye Contact

Look directly into the camera when speaking to simulate eye contact.

6. Posture

Sit up straight and lean slightly forward to show engagement.

7. Nodding and Smiling

Use these cues more deliberately in virtual settings to show you're listening and engaged.

Cultural Considerations in Body Language

It's important to remember that body language can vary significantly across cultures.

- Research cultural norms if you're interviewing with a company from a different cultural background
- Be aware that gestures considered positive in one culture may be offensive in another
- When in doubt, mirror the body language of your interviewer

Practicing and Improving Your Body Language

Like any skill, mastering body language requires practice.

1. Record Yourself: Video yourself in mock interviews to observe your body language.
2. Seek Feedback: Ask friends or mentors to give you honest feedback on your nonverbal communication.
3. Practice in Low-Stakes Situations: Use everyday interactions as opportunities to practice your body language skills.
4. Stay Relaxed: Remember that tension can negatively impact your body language. Use relaxation techniques before important interactions.

Conclusion

Mastering nonverbal communication is a powerful tool in your professional arsenal. By being mindful of your body language and adept at reading the cues of others, you can significantly enhance your ability to connect, persuade, and succeed in professional settings.

Remember, the goal is not to adopt a rigid set of behaviors, but to develop a natural, confident presence that aligns with your verbal communication. With practice, these body language techniques will become second nature, allowing you to focus on the content of your interactions while your nonverbal cues work in harmony to present your best professional self.

As you continue your job search and career journey, make conscious efforts to implement these body language secrets. You'll likely find that as your nonverbal communication skills improve, so too does your overall effectiveness in professional interactions, from networking events to job interviews and beyond.

Chapter 8: Answering Common Questions with the STAR Method

In the landscape of modern job interviews, behavioral questions have become increasingly prevalent. These questions ask you to recount specific situations from your past experiences to demonstrate your skills and problem-solving abilities. One of the most effective techniques for answering these questions is the STAR method. In this chapter, we'll explore how to master this technique to provide compelling, structured responses that showcase your capabilities.

Understanding the STAR Method

STAR is an acronym that stands for:

- **Situation**: Set the context for your story.
- **Task**: Describe the challenge or responsibility you faced.
- **Action**: Explain the specific steps you took to address the task.
- **Result**: Share the outcomes of your actions.

This method provides a clear, concise structure for your answers, ensuring you cover all the essential elements of your experience without rambling or missing crucial details.

CHAPTER 8: ANSWERING COMMON QUESTIONS WITH THE STAR METHOD

Why Use the STAR Method?

1. **Structure**: It provides a logical flow to your answers.
2. **Completeness**: It ensures you cover all aspects of the situation.
3. **Conciseness**: It helps you stay focused and avoid irrelevant details.
4. **Measurability**: It emphasizes concrete results and outcomes.
5. **Preparation**: It allows you to prepare and practice your responses effectively.

Implementing the STAR Method

Let's break down each component of the STAR method and explore how to implement it effectively.

Situation

Start by setting the scene. Provide context for your story, but keep it brief.

- When and where did this event occur?
- What was your role?
- Who else was involved?

Example: "In my previous role as a project manager at XYZ Corp, we were facing a critical deadline for a major client project."

Task

Describe the challenge or responsibility you faced in this situation.

- What was expected of you?
- What difficulties or obstacles did you encounter?

Example: "My task was to ensure the project was completed on time and within budget, despite unexpected technical challenges that had put us behind schedule."

Action

This is the most crucial part of your answer. Detail the specific steps you took to address the task.

- What did you do?
- How did you do it?
- Why did you choose this course of action?

Example: "I immediately called a team meeting to reassess our timeline and resources. I redistributed tasks based on team members' strengths and implemented daily stand-up meetings to improve communication. Additionally, I negotiated with our client for a small extension on less critical deliverables, allowing us to focus on key components."

Result

Conclude by sharing the outcomes of your actions. Where possible, quantify your results.

- What was the outcome of your actions?
- How did it impact the company or team?
- What did you learn from this experience?

Example: "As a result of these actions, we successfully delivered the project just one day past the original deadline, which the client accepted without penalty. The project came in 2% under budget, and the client was so impressed with our communication and problem-solving that they awarded us two additional projects the following quarter."

CHAPTER 8: ANSWERING COMMON QUESTIONS WITH THE STAR METHOD

Common Behavioral Questions and STAR Responses

Let's apply the STAR method to some common behavioral interview questions:

1. "Tell me about a time when you had to work under pressure."

S: During my internship at a busy marketing agency, we unexpectedly lost a key team member right before a major campaign launch.

T: I was tasked with taking over their responsibilities to ensure the campaign launched on time.

A: I quickly familiarized myself with the project details, working extra hours to get up to speed. I prioritized tasks, delegated where possible, and maintained clear communication with the team and client.

R: We successfully launched the campaign on schedule. The client was pleased with the results, and my manager commended my ability to step up under pressure.

2. "Describe a situation where you had to resolve a conflict with a coworker."

S: In my role as a software developer, I disagreed with a colleague over the best approach to a complex coding problem.

T: We needed to find a solution that satisfied both of our concerns without delaying the project.

A: I suggested we meet privately to discuss our viewpoints. I actively listened to my colleague's perspective and shared my own reasoning. We then brainstormed a hybrid approach that incorporated the strengths of both our ideas.

R: Our combined solution was more robust than either of our original proposals. This experience improved our working relationship and led to more collaborative problem-solving in future projects.

Tips for Mastering the STAR Method

1. **Prepare in Advance**: Identify key experiences from your career that demonstrate important skills like leadership, problem-solving, and teamwork. Develop STAR stories for each.
2. **Be Specific**: Use concrete details and avoid generalizations. Instead of saying "I improved efficiency," say "I increased team productivity by 25% over three months."
3. **Keep it Relevant**: Choose examples that closely relate to the job you're applying for.
4. **Be Honest**: Don't exaggerate or fabricate stories. Authenticity is key.
5. **Practice, But Don't Memorize**: While it's good to practice your STAR stories, avoid memorizing them word-for-word. This can make your answers sound rehearsed and unnatural.
6. **Keep it Concise**: Aim to keep your STAR answers to about 2-3 minutes.
7. **Focus on Your Role**: While you may have worked as part of a team, focus on your specific contributions and actions.
8. **Highlight Growth**: If the outcome wasn't entirely positive, focus on what you learned and how you've grown from the experience.

Adapting the STAR Method

While STAR is an excellent framework, remember to be flexible. Some variations include:

- **CAR (Context, Action, Result)**: Similar to STAR, but combines Situation and Task.
- **SOAR (Situation, Obstacle, Action, Result)**: Emphasizes the challenge you faced.
- **PARADE (Problem, Anticipated consequence, Role, Action, Decision, Evaluation)**: A more detailed framework for complex situations.

Choose the variation that best fits the question and your experience.

Common Pitfalls to Avoid

1. **Lack of Preparation**: Not having STAR stories ready can lead to rambling or incomplete answers.
2. **Choosing Weak Examples**: Ensure your stories demonstrate significant challenges and impactful results.
3. **Focusing Too Much on the Situation**: Spend more time on your actions and results.
4. **Neglecting the Result**: Always conclude with the outcome, even if it's a lesson learned from a less-than-ideal result.
5. **One-Size-Fits-All Approach**: Tailor your STAR stories to the specific job and company.

Conclusion

The STAR method is a powerful tool for answering behavioral interview questions effectively. By providing a clear structure for your responses, it allows you to showcase your skills and experiences in a compelling, concise manner. Remember, the key to mastering this technique lies in preparation and practice.

As you prepare for your interviews, develop a repertoire of STAR stories that highlight your key strengths and align with common job requirements. Practice delivering these stories naturally, adapting them as needed for different questions and contexts.

With time and practice, the STAR method will become second nature, allowing you to confidently navigate behavioral interviews and effectively demonstrate your value to potential employers. By mastering this technique, you'll be well-equipped to showcase your experiences and skills, setting yourself apart as a strong, capable candidate in any interview situation.

Chapter 9: Tackling Behavioral Questions Like a Pro

Behavioral questions have become a cornerstone of modern interview techniques. These questions are designed to elicit specific examples of how you've handled situations in the past, providing interviewers with insights into your skills, decision-making process, and potential future performance. While the STAR method provides an excellent framework for answering these questions, this chapter will delve deeper into strategies for tackling behavioral questions like a true professional.

Understanding the Psychology Behind Behavioral Questions

Before we dive into advanced techniques, it's crucial to understand why interviewers ask behavioral questions:

1. **Past Behavior Predicts Future Performance**: Interviewers believe that how you've acted in the past is a good indicator of how you'll perform in the future.
2. **Assessing Soft Skills**: These questions help evaluate crucial soft skills like communication, leadership, problem-solving, and teamwork.
3. **Cultural Fit**: Your responses can indicate whether your values and work style align with the company culture.
4. **Stress Testing**: Some behavioral questions are designed to see how you handle pressure or challenging situations.

Understanding these motivations can help you frame your responses more effectively.

Advanced STAR Techniques

While we covered the basics of the STAR method in the previous chapter, here are some advanced techniques to elevate your responses:

1. The Hook

Start your STAR story with a compelling hook that grabs the interviewer's attention.

Example: "The day our biggest client threatened to leave taught me the true meaning of customer service."

2. Quantify Your Results

Whenever possible, use specific numbers to illustrate your impact.

Example: "This strategy increased customer retention by 35% and boosted annual revenue by $500,000."

3. Highlight Growth

Even if the outcome wasn't perfect, emphasize what you learned and how you've applied that knowledge since.

Example: "While we missed the deadline by two days, I learned the importance of buffer time in project planning. I've since implemented a 20% time buffer in all my projects, and haven't missed a deadline since."

4. Bridge to the Job

Connect your story explicitly to the role you're applying for.

  Example: "This experience in crisis management would be directly applicable to the challenges faced in the position we're discussing today."

Preparing Your Behavioral Question Arsenal

To truly tackle behavioral questions like a pro, you need a well-prepared arsenal of stories. Here's how to build it:

1. Job Analysis

Carefully analyze the job description and company values. Identify the key skills and qualities they're looking for.

2. Story Mining

Reflect on your experiences and identify stories that demonstrate these key skills. Aim for a mix of successes, challenges overcome, and learning experiences.

3. Story Mapping

Create a matrix mapping your stories to common behavioral questions and key skills. This will help you quickly recall relevant stories during the interview.

4. Adaptability

Practice adapting your core stories to answer different types of questions. One story might be tweaked to demonstrate leadership, problem-solving, or teamwork, depending on the question.

CHAPTER 9: TACKLING BEHAVIORAL QUESTIONS LIKE A PRO

Advanced Behavioral Question Strategies

1. The Reverse Engineered Response

If you don't have a perfect story that matches the question, use this technique:

1. Identify the skill or quality the question is probing for.
2. Think of a time you demonstrated that quality, even if the situation doesn't perfectly match the question.
3. Frame your response to emphasize the relevant aspects of your experience.

Example Question: "Tell me about a time you had to persuade a group to accept an unpopular idea." You might not have this exact experience, but you could share a story about building consensus in a team, emphasizing the persuasion aspects.

2. The Hypothetical Bridge

If you truly lack experience in a particular area:

1. Acknowledge your lack of direct experience.
2. Discuss how you would hypothetically handle the situation.
3. Bridge to a related experience that demonstrates relevant skills.

Example: "While I haven't faced that exact situation, here's how I would approach it... In fact, I used a similar approach when..."

3. The Meta-Analysis

Sometimes, analyzing your thought process can be as valuable as the story itself:

1. Share your story using the STAR method.
2. Then, explain why you chose that particular approach.
3. Discuss what other options you considered and why you didn't choose them.

This demonstrates your analytical skills and decision-making process.

4. The Culture Connect

Align your response with the company's values and culture:

1. Research the company's core values before the interview.
2. In your responses, subtly emphasize aspects that align with these values.

Example: If the company values innovation, highlight the creative aspects of your problem-solving approach.

Handling Challenging Behavioral Questions

Some behavioral questions are designed to be challenging. Here's how to handle them:

1. Negative Experience Questions

Examples: "Tell me about a time you failed" or "Describe a conflict with a coworker"
   Strategy:

- Be honest about the challenging situation.
- Focus on what you learned and how you've grown.
- Explain how you've applied these lessons successfully since then.

2. Ethical Dilemma Questions

Example: "Describe a situation where you had to make an ethical decision"
Strategy:

- Demonstrate your decision-making process.
- Emphasize your commitment to integrity.
- Explain how you balance competing interests.

3. Pressure Situation Questions

Example: "Tell me about a time you had to work under extremely close supervision or extremely loose supervision"
Strategy:

- Stay positive, avoid criticizing past employers or colleagues.
- Focus on how you adapted your work style to the situation.
- Highlight your flexibility and ability to thrive in different environments.

The Art of Storytelling in Behavioral Responses

Remember, your goal isn't just to answer the question, but to tell a compelling story that showcases your skills and leaves a lasting impression.

1. **Structure**: Use a clear beginning, middle, and end.
2. **Detail**: Provide enough detail to make your story vivid, but not so much that you lose focus.
3. **Emotion**: Don't be afraid to convey the emotions you felt during the experience. This adds authenticity to your story.
4. **Pacing**: Practice your delivery to ensure you maintain a good pace, neither rushing nor dragging.
5. **Relevance**: Every detail you include should serve a purpose in demonstrating your skills or qualities.

Practice Makes Perfect

The key to tackling behavioral questions like a pro is practice:

1. **Mock Interviews**: Conduct mock interviews with friends, family, or career counselors.
2. **Record Yourself**: Video record your responses to analyze your body language and delivery.
3. **Seek Feedback**: Ask for honest feedback on your responses and refine them accordingly.
4. **Continuous Improvement**: After each real interview, reflect on how you answered behavioral questions and identify areas for improvement.

Conclusion

Mastering behavioral questions is a crucial skill in today's job market. By understanding the psychology behind these questions, preparing a robust arsenal of stories, and employing advanced techniques, you can transform these challenging questions into opportunities to showcase your unique value as a candidate.

Remember, the goal isn't to have a perfectly scripted answer for every possible question, but to become adept at drawing from your experiences to demonstrate your skills and qualities. With practice and the strategies outlined in this chapter, you'll be well-equipped to tackle any behavioral question that comes your way, impressing interviewers with your thoughtful, structured, and compelling responses.

As you continue to gain new experiences in your career, don't forget to update your story arsenal. Each new challenge you face and problem you solve is a potential answer to a future behavioral question. By continuously reflecting on your experiences and the lessons learned, you'll not only become better at answering these questions but also grow as a professional.

Chapter 10: Navigating Tricky Situational Questions

While behavioral questions ask about past experiences, situational questions pose hypothetical scenarios to assess how you would handle potential future challenges. These questions can be particularly tricky as they often involve complex scenarios with no clear-cut answers. In this chapter, we'll explore strategies for navigating these challenging questions with confidence and professionalism.

Understanding Situational Questions

Situational questions typically begin with phrases like:

- "What would you do if…"
- "How would you handle…"
- "Imagine that…"

The key difference from behavioral questions is that situational questions are forward-looking and hypothetical, while behavioral questions are backward-looking and based on actual experiences.

The Purpose of Situational Questions

Interviewers use situational questions to:

1. Assess your problem-solving skills
2. Evaluate your ability to think on your feet
3. Gauge your alignment with company values and culture
4. Understand your decision-making process
5. Explore how you might handle challenges specific to the role

Strategies for Tackling Situational Questions

1. The STAR Method Adaptation

While the STAR method is primarily for behavioral questions, you can adapt it for situational questions:

- Situation: Restate the hypothetical scenario to ensure understanding
- Task: Identify the core challenge or goal in the scenario
- Action: Describe the steps you would take to address the situation
- Result: Predict the potential outcomes of your actions

2. The "Experience Bridge"

If the hypothetical scenario reminds you of a real experience:

1. Briefly outline how you would approach the hypothetical situation
2. Then say, "In fact, I faced a similar situation in my previous role..."
3. Describe the real situation using the STAR method
4. Conclude by relating it back to the hypothetical scenario

This approach combines the strengths of both situational and behavioral responses.

3. The "Values and Principles" Approach

When faced with an ethical dilemma or complex scenario:

1. Identify the core principles or values at stake
2. Explain how you would balance these considerations
3. Outline your decision-making process
4. Describe the actions you would take

This approach demonstrates your ethical reasoning and decision-making skills.

4. The "Step-by-Step" Method

For complex scenarios:

1. Break down the situation into smaller, manageable parts
2. Address each part systematically
3. Explain your reasoning at each step

This showcases your analytical skills and methodical approach to problem-solving.

5. The "Multiple Perspectives" Technique

For scenarios involving multiple stakeholders:

1. Identify all the parties involved
2. Consider the perspective and needs of each stakeholder
3. Propose a solution that balances these different interests
4. Explain how you would communicate your decision to each party

This demonstrates your ability to see the big picture and manage complex interpersonal dynamics.

Handling Specific Types of Situational Questions

1. Ethical Dilemmas

Example: "What would you do if you discovered your supervisor was violating company policy?"
Approach:

- Acknowledge the sensitivity of the situation
- Emphasize the importance of integrity and company policies
- Outline a step-by-step approach (e.g., gathering facts, consulting HR or ethics hotline)
- Stress the importance of professionalism and discretion

2. Conflict Resolution

Example: "How would you handle a disagreement with a coworker on a critical project decision?"
Approach:

- Emphasize the importance of open communication
- Describe a process for understanding both perspectives
- Suggest finding common ground or a compromise
- Mention the possibility of involving a mediator if necessary
- Stress the importance of maintaining a positive working relationship

3. Crisis Management

Example: "What would you do if a major client threatened to leave due to a product failure?"
Approach:

- Emphasize the need for quick but thoughtful action
- Outline steps: gathering information, assembling a response team, developing a solution
- Discuss how you would communicate with the client
- Mention the importance of learning from the situation to prevent future occurrences

4. Leadership Challenges

Example: "How would you motivate a team that's falling behind on its targets?"
Approach:

- Stress the importance of understanding the root causes
- Suggest a combination of team and individual discussions
- Propose strategies like setting clearer goals, providing additional resources, or adjusting processes
- Emphasize the importance of positive reinforcement and recognition

5. Innovation and Adaptability

Example: "How would you approach implementing a major change in company processes that you expect will face resistance?"
Approach:

- Emphasize the importance of clear communication about the reasons for change
- Suggest involving team members in the planning process
- Propose a phased implementation approach
- Discuss strategies for addressing concerns and resistance
- Mention the importance of celebrating small wins along the way

Tips for Excelling at Situational Questions

1. **Practice Active Listening**: Ensure you fully understand the question before responding.
2. **Take Your Time**: It's okay to pause briefly to collect your thoughts before answering.
3. **Ask Clarifying Questions**: If the scenario is unclear, don't hesitate to ask for more details.
4. **Stay Calm**: Some questions are designed to be stressful. Maintain your composure.
5. **Be Consistent**: Ensure your answers align with the values and skills you've emphasized throughout the interview.
6. **Show Flexibility**: Demonstrate that you can adapt your approach based on new information or changing circumstances.
7. **Emphasize Soft Skills**: Situational questions are great opportunities to showcase skills like communication, teamwork, and leadership.
8. **Follow Up**: After describing your approach, explain how you would assess its effectiveness and make adjustments if needed.

Preparing for Situational Questions

While you can't predict every possible scenario, you can prepare effectively:

1. **Research Common Scenarios**: Look up typical situational questions for your industry and role.
2. **Understand the Job**: Anticipate challenges you might face in the position you're applying for.
3. **Know the Company**: Research the company's values, culture, and current challenges.
4. **Reflect on Your Experiences**: Even if you haven't faced the exact scenarios, think about similar challenges you've overcome.
5. **Practice Frameworks**: Get comfortable with problem-solving frameworks that you can apply to various situations.

Conclusion

Navigating tricky situational questions is as much about your thought process as it is about your final answer. Interviewers are often more interested in how you approach a problem than in the specific solution you propose.

By employing the strategies outlined in this chapter, you can transform these challenging questions into opportunities to showcase your critical thinking, problem-solving skills, and alignment with the company's values. Remember, there's often no single "right" answer to these questions. What matters is demonstrating a thoughtful, ethical, and structured approach to tackling complex scenarios.

As you prepare for your interviews, practice applying these techniques to a variety of hypothetical situations. The more comfortable you become with this type of question, the more confidently you'll be able to navigate whatever scenarios the interviewer presents.

Ultimately, your ability to handle situational questions effectively can set you apart as a candidate who's not only qualified for the current role but also has the potential to tackle future challenges and grow within the organization. Approach these questions as opportunities to shine, and you'll be well on your way to interview success.

Chapter 11: Showcasing Your Soft Skills Effectively

In today's competitive job market, technical skills and qualifications are often just the entry point. What truly sets candidates apart are their soft skills - the personal attributes that enable someone to interact effectively and harmoniously with others. This chapter will explore how to effectively showcase your soft skills during the job interview process, helping you stand out as a well-rounded, valuable candidate.

Understanding Soft Skills

Soft skills, also known as interpersonal or people skills, are personal attributes that characterize your relationships with others. They include:

1. Communication
2. Teamwork
3. Adaptability
4. Problem-solving
5. Critical thinking
6. Time management
7. Leadership
8. Creativity
9. Emotional intelligence
10. Work ethic

CHAPTER 11: SHOWCASING YOUR SOFT SKILLS EFFECTIVELY

Unlike hard skills, which are teachable and measurable abilities like coding or accounting, soft skills are more subjective and harder to quantify. However, they are equally, if not more, important in determining your success in a role.

Why Soft Skills Matter

Employers value soft skills because:

1. They are transferable across industries and roles
2. They contribute to a positive work environment
3. They enhance productivity and collaboration
4. They are crucial for leadership positions
5. They are harder to teach than technical skills

Identifying Your Soft Skills

Before you can effectively showcase your soft skills, you need to identify your strengths. Here's how:

1. **Self-reflection**: Think about past experiences where you excelled in interpersonal situations.
2. **Feedback**: Ask colleagues, supervisors, or mentors about your strengths.
3. **Personality assessments**: Tools like Myers-Briggs or StrengthsFinder can provide insights.
4. **Job description analysis**: Identify the soft skills emphasized in job postings in your field.

Strategies for Showcasing Soft Skills

1. Show, Don't Tell

Instead of simply stating you have a skill, demonstrate it through specific examples.

Bad: "I'm a great communicator." Good: "In my previous role, I bridged communication between the technical team and non-technical stakeholders, which led to a 20% increase in client satisfaction."

2. Use the STAR Method

Adapt the STAR method to highlight soft skills:

- Situation: Set the context
- Task: Describe the challenge
- Action: Explain how you used your soft skills
- Result: Share the positive outcome

Example: "In my last team project (Situation), we faced conflicting opinions on project direction (Task). I organized a team meeting, ensured everyone's voice was heard, and facilitated a compromise (Action). As a result, we completed the project on time with high team morale (Result)."

3. Incorporate Soft Skills into Your Responses

Weave mentions of soft skills naturally into your answers to various interview questions.

Question: "Tell me about yourself." Response: "I'm a marketing professional with five years of experience. Throughout my career, I've developed strong communication skills, allowing me to effectively collaborate with diverse teams and present complex ideas to clients in an accessible way."

4. Provide Quantifiable Results

Where possible, quantify the results of using your soft skills.
   Example: "My ability to build strong client relationships resulted in a 30% increase in repeat business last year."

5. Use Power Words

Incorporate words that imply soft skills:

- Collaborated (Teamwork)
- Innovated (Creativity)
- Mentored (Leadership)
- Resolved (Problem-solving)
- Prioritized (Time management)

6. Demonstrate Skills in Real-Time

Use the interview itself as an opportunity to showcase your soft skills:

- Communication: Articulate your answers clearly and listen actively
- Adaptability: Respond positively to unexpected questions
- Time management: Arrive on time and manage the length of your responses
- Emotional intelligence: Read and respond appropriately to the interviewer's cues

Showcasing Specific Soft Skills

Let's explore how to highlight some key soft skills:

1. Communication

- Articulate your thoughts clearly and concisely
- Provide examples of written communication (e.g., reports, presentations)
- Discuss how you've bridged communication gaps in past roles

2. Teamwork

- Share stories of successful collaborations
- Highlight your role in team achievements
- Discuss how you handle team conflicts

3. Adaptability

- Provide examples of how you've dealt with change
- Discuss your approach to learning new skills
- Share a story of overcoming an unexpected challenge

4. Problem-solving

- Walk the interviewer through your problem-solving process
- Provide examples of creative solutions you've developed
- Discuss how you approach complex or ambiguous problems

5. Leadership

- Share experiences of leading projects or teams
- Discuss how you motivate and inspire others
- Provide examples of mentoring or developing team members

Tailoring Soft Skills to the Job

Different roles may prioritize different soft skills. Here's how to tailor your approach:

1. **Analyze the job description**: Identify the soft skills emphasized in the posting.
2. **Research the company culture**: Understand what interpersonal qualities they value.
3. **Consider the role's requirements**: A customer service role might prioritize communication and empathy, while a project management position might emphasize leadership and time management.
4. **Prepare relevant examples**: Focus on experiences that highlight the most relevant soft skills for the role.

Addressing Soft Skill Weaknesses

If asked about areas for improvement:

1. Be honest about skills you're working to develop
2. Explain the steps you're taking to improve
3. Provide an example of progress you've made

Example: "I'm working on improving my public speaking skills. I've joined a local Toastmasters club and have already seen improvement in my ability to present ideas confidently to groups."

Continuous Soft Skill Development

Showcase your commitment to growth by discussing how you continually develop your soft skills:

- Mention relevant books, podcasts, or courses

- Discuss your participation in workshops or seminars
- Share how you seek out and apply feedback

Conclusion

Effectively showcasing your soft skills can significantly enhance your appeal as a candidate. By providing concrete examples, quantifying results where possible, and demonstrating these skills throughout the interview process, you paint a picture of a well-rounded professional who can not only do the job but can also positively impact the team and organization.

Remember, soft skills are not just buzzwords to sprinkle throughout your interview. They are fundamental attributes that define how you work and interact with others. By authentically sharing experiences that highlight these skills, you allow the interviewer to envision the value you'll bring to the role beyond just your technical capabilities.

As you prepare for your interviews, take time to reflect on your experiences and identify strong examples that demonstrate your soft skills. Practice articulating these examples clearly and concisely. And most importantly, approach the interview as an opportunity to genuinely connect with the interviewer, showcasing in real-time the interpersonal skills that make you an outstanding candidate.

By effectively showcasing your soft skills, you differentiate yourself from other candidates and position yourself as a well-rounded, valuable asset to any team. In a job market where technical skills are often similar among candidates, your soft skills can be the deciding factor that lands you the job.

Chapter 12: Technical Interview Strategies (for relevant fields)

Technical interviews are a crucial part of the hiring process for many fields, including software development, data science, engineering, and other technology-related roles. These interviews are designed to assess your technical skills, problem-solving abilities, and how you approach complex challenges. In this chapter, we'll explore strategies to help you prepare for and excel in technical interviews across various fields.

Understanding the Technical Interview Process

Technical interviews can vary widely depending on the company and role, but they often include:

1. Coding challenges
2. Algorithm and data structure questions
3. System design problems
4. Domain-specific knowledge questions
5. Behavioral questions in a technical context

The goal is not just to test your knowledge, but to understand your thought process, problem-solving approach, and ability to communicate technical concepts.

General Preparation Strategies

1. Review Fundamentals

Regardless of your experience level, revisit the basics:

- Core concepts in your field
- Common algorithms and data structures
- Design patterns relevant to your domain

2. Practice Coding

For software-related roles:

- Solve coding problems on platforms like LeetCode, HackerRank, or CodeSignal
- Practice writing clean, efficient code
- Get comfortable coding on a whiteboard or in a simple text editor

3. Study System Design

For more senior roles:

- Practice designing scalable systems
- Understand trade-offs in system architecture
- Be familiar with common technologies and their use cases

4. Mock Interviews

- Conduct mock interviews with peers or mentors
- Use platforms like Pramp for peer-to-peer mock interviews
- Practice explaining your thought process out loud

5. Research the Company

- Understand the company's tech stack
- Read their engineering blog if available
- Be familiar with their products or services

Strategies for Different Types of Technical Questions

1. Coding Challenges

Approach: a) Clarify the problem and requirements b) Discuss your approach before coding c) Start with a simple solution, then optimize d) Test your code with various inputs e) Analyze time and space complexity

Example: "Given an array of integers, find two numbers such that they add up to a specific target number."

Approach demonstration: "First, I'd clarify if the array is sorted and if we need to handle any edge cases. Assuming it's unsorted and we need to find the indices, I'd start with a brute force approach using nested loops. Then, I'd optimize it using a hash map to achieve O(n) time complexity. Let me code this solution…"

2. Algorithm and Data Structure Questions

Approach: a) Identify the type of problem (e.g., searching, sorting, graph) b) Consider multiple approaches c) Explain trade-offs between different solutions d) Implement the most appropriate solution

Example: "Implement a function to check if a binary tree is balanced."

Approach demonstration: "I'd approach this recursively. We'll define a balanced tree as one where the heights of the two subtrees of any node never differ by more than one. I'll implement a helper function that returns the height of a subtree, or -1 if it's unbalanced. This gives us O(n) time complexity as we only need to visit each node once. Let me code this solution…"

3. System Design Problems

Approach: a) Clarify requirements and constraints b) Start with a high-level design c) Dive into specific components d) Discuss scalability and potential bottlenecks e) Consider trade-offs in your design choices

Example: "Design a URL shortening service like bit.ly."

Approach demonstration: "Let's start by clarifying the requirements. We need to generate short URLs, redirect users, and handle high traffic. For the high-level design, we'll need a web server, a database, and a caching layer. Let's discuss each component in detail..."

4. Domain-Specific Knowledge Questions

Approach: a) Provide a clear, concise definition b) Offer an example or use case c) Discuss any relevant trade-offs or limitations

Example: "Explain the difference between HTTP and HTTPS."

Approach demonstration: "HTTP, or Hypertext Transfer Protocol, is the foundation of data communication on the web. HTTPS is the secure version of HTTP. The main difference is that HTTPS uses SSL/TLS protocol for encryption and authentication. This means that data exchanged between the client and server is encrypted, providing protection against eavesdropping and tampering. An example of HTTPS usage is in online banking..."

Communication Strategies

Effective communication is crucial in technical interviews. Here are some strategies:

1. **Think Aloud**: Verbalize your thought process as you work through problems.
2. **Clarify Assumptions**: Always clarify the problem requirements and any assumptions you're making.
3. **Structured Responses**: Use a consistent structure for your answers,

especially for system design questions.
4. **Use Analogies**: When explaining complex concepts, use analogies to make them more understandable.
5. **Ask Questions**: Don't hesitate to ask for clarification or hints if you're stuck.
6. **Admit Knowledge Gaps**: If you don't know something, be honest and explain how you'd find the answer.

Handling Difficult Situations

1. **When You're Stuck**:

- Take a deep breath and stay calm
- Break down the problem into smaller parts
- Consider edge cases or simplifications
- Ask for a hint if needed

1. **Receiving Feedback**:

- Listen carefully to the interviewer's feedback
- Be open to suggestions and alternative approaches
- Demonstrate your ability to learn and adapt quickly

1. **Time Management**:

- If you're running out of time, explain how you'd complete the problem
- Discuss optimizations or improvements you'd make with more time

Field-Specific Advice

Software Development

- Be prepared to discuss different programming paradigms
- Understand software development methodologies (Agile, Scrum, etc.)
- Be familiar with version control systems like Git

Data Science

- Be prepared to discuss statistical concepts and machine learning algorithms
- Practice explaining complex analytical concepts to non-technical audiences
- Be ready to work with real-world, messy datasets

DevOps/SRE

- Understand cloud platforms and containerization technologies
- Be familiar with CI/CD pipelines and infrastructure as code
- Be prepared to discuss incident response and system reliability

Embedded Systems

- Understand hardware constraints and optimization techniques
- Be familiar with real-time operating systems and interrupt handling
- Be prepared to discuss low-level programming concepts

Post-Interview Strategies

1. **Self-Reflection**: After the interview, reflect on what went well and areas for improvement.
2. **Follow-Up**: Send a thank-you email, reiterating your interest in the position.
3. **Continuous Learning**: Use the interview experience to guide your

further learning and preparation.

Conclusion

Technical interviews can be challenging, but with the right preparation and mindset, they're an opportunity to showcase your skills and problem-solving abilities. Remember, interviewers are not just assessing your current knowledge, but your potential to learn and grow within their organization.

Key takeaways:

1. Thoroughly prepare by reviewing fundamentals and practicing regularly
2. Communicate clearly and effectively throughout the interview
3. Stay calm and methodical when approaching problems
4. Be honest about your knowledge and show a willingness to learn
5. Use each interview as a learning experience to improve your skills

By applying these strategies and continuously refining your technical skills, you'll be well-equipped to tackle even the most challenging technical interviews. Remember, the goal is not just to get the right answer, but to demonstrate your problem-solving approach, technical communication skills, and passion for your field. With practice and persistence, you'll be well on your way to landing your dream technical role.

Chapter 13: Remote Interview Success: Mastering Virtual Platforms

The rise of remote work has transformed the hiring landscape, making virtual interviews increasingly common. Whether conducted via Zoom, Skype, Google Meet, or other platforms, remote interviews present unique challenges and opportunities. This chapter will guide you through the process of mastering virtual platforms to ensure your remote interview success.

Understanding the Virtual Interview Landscape

Remote interviews can take various forms:

1. One-on-one video calls
2. Panel interviews with multiple interviewers
3. Pre-recorded video responses
4. Virtual assessment centers
5. Technical interviews with screen sharing

Each format requires specific preparation and strategies.

Technical Preparation

1. Choose the Right Equipment

- Camera: Ensure your device has a good quality camera. External webcams often provide better quality than built-in laptop cameras.
- Microphone: Use a clear, reliable microphone. Consider investing in an external mic for better audio quality.
- Lighting: Ensure you're well-lit, ideally with natural light facing you or a ring light.

2. Master the Platform

- Familiarize yourself with the specific platform (Zoom, Skype, etc.) before the interview.
- Test your audio and video settings in advance.
- Learn how to share your screen if required for technical interviews.
- Understand how to troubleshoot common issues.

3. Ensure a Stable Internet Connection

- Test your internet speed before the interview.
- Consider using a wired connection for more stability.
- Have a backup plan (e.g., mobile hotspot) in case of connection issues.

4. Set Up Your Space

- Choose a quiet, well-lit location with a neutral background.
- Ensure your background is professional and clutter-free.
- Consider using a virtual background if your space isn't ideal.

Presentation Skills for Virtual Interviews

1. Eye Contact

- Look directly into the camera when speaking to simulate eye contact.
- Position your camera at eye level for the most flattering angle.

2. Body Language

- Sit up straight and lean slightly forward to show engagement.
- Use hand gestures deliberately and keep them in frame.
- Nod and smile to show active listening.

3. Vocal Techniques

- Speak clearly and at a moderate pace.
- Use pauses effectively to emphasize points.
- Modulate your tone to maintain interest.

4. Dress Appropriately

- Dress professionally from head to toe (in case you need to stand up).
- Avoid busy patterns or bright colors that may be distracting on camera.

Engaging with Interviewers Virtually

1. Active Listening

- Use verbal and non-verbal cues to show you're listening.
- Nod, smile, and use brief affirmations like "I see" or "Yes, I understand."

2. Managing Interruptions

- Wait a beat before speaking to avoid talking over the interviewer.
- If you're interrupted, pause gracefully and allow the interviewer to speak.

3. Asking Questions

- Prepare thoughtful questions about the role and company.
- Use the chat function to note down questions as they occur to you during the interview.

4. Building Rapport

- Start with small talk to establish a connection.
- Show enthusiasm through your tone and facial expressions.

Handling Technical Difficulties

1. Stay Calm

- If you encounter technical issues, remain professional and calm.
- Have the interviewer's contact information handy in case you need to switch to a phone call.

2. Have a Backup Plan

- Know how to quickly switch to your phone's hotspot if your primary internet fails.
- Have the interview platform's mobile app installed on your phone as a backup.

3. Addressing Issues Proactively

- If you're having trouble hearing or seeing the interviewer, politely let them know.
- If your video freezes, switch it off and on again quickly.

Strategies for Specific Virtual Interview Formats

1. One-on-One Video Calls

- Focus on building a personal connection.
- Use the interviewer's name occasionally to personalize the conversation.

2. Panel Interviews

- Address each interviewer by name when answering their specific questions.
- Make eye contact with the camera to engage all panelists.

3. Pre-Recorded Video Responses

- Practice your responses to common questions beforehand.
- Speak with energy and enthusiasm, even though you're not talking to a live person.

4. Virtual Assessment Centers

- Be prepared for breakout rooms and group activities.
- Show leadership and teamwork skills in virtual group exercises.

5. Technical Interviews with Screen Sharing

- Practice sharing your screen and navigating between windows smoothly.
- Ensure your desktop is clean and professional if you need to share it.

Pre-Interview Preparation

1. Test Run

- Conduct a mock interview with a friend using the same platform.
- Record yourself to review your presentation and background.

2. Prepare Your Environment

- Inform household members about your interview to ensure quiet.
- Close unnecessary programs on your computer to avoid notifications.

3. Have Materials Ready

- Keep a copy of your resume, the job description, and prepared notes nearby.
- Have a glass of water within reach.

Post-Interview Follow-Up

1. Send a Thank-You Email

- Reference specific points from the conversation to personalize your message.
- Reiterate your interest in the position and company.

2. Address Any Technical Issues

- If there were any significant technical problems, briefly apologize and offer to provide any additional information if needed.

Leveraging the Advantages of Virtual Interviews

1. Use Notes Strategically

- Keep brief notes out of frame to reference during the interview.
- Don't rely too heavily on notes – maintain natural eye contact and engagement.

2. Showcase Your Remote Work Skills

- Highlight your ability to communicate effectively in a virtual environment.
- Discuss any experience with remote work or virtual collaboration tools.

3. Demonstrate Tech-Savviness

- Your ability to navigate the virtual interview process smoothly showcases valuable digital skills.

Common Virtual Interview Mistakes to Avoid

1. Poor lighting or camera angles
2. Distracting backgrounds
3. Looking at the screen instead of the camera
4. Forgetting to mute when necessary
5. Dressing inappropriately (e.g., overly casual or distracting patterns)
6. Not testing technology in advance
7. Allowing interruptions from notifications or household members

Conclusion

Mastering virtual platforms for remote interviews is an essential skill in today's job market. By thoroughly preparing your technology, environment, and presentation skills, you can transform the potential challenges of virtual interviews into opportunities to showcase your adaptability and digital competence.

Remember, the core principles of interviewing still apply in a virtual setting. Be prepared, professional, and engaged. Your ability to navigate the virtual interview process effectively can itself be a strong selling point, demonstrating your readiness for the modern workplace.

As you practice these strategies, you'll become more comfortable with the virtual interview format, allowing your true skills and personality to shine through. Embrace the unique aspects of remote interviews, such as the ability to reference notes or showcase your home office setup, while maintaining the professionalism and connection of an in-person meeting.

With these tools and strategies at your disposal, you're well-equipped to ace your next virtual interview and take the next step in your career journey. Good luck!

Chapter 14: Group Interview Dynamics: Standing Out in a Crowd

Group interviews can be intimidating. You're not only trying to impress the interviewer but also competing directly with other candidates. However, with the right strategies, you can turn this challenging format into an opportunity to showcase your unique strengths. This chapter will guide you through the dynamics of group interviews and provide strategies to help you stand out positively.

Understanding Group Interviews

Group interviews typically take two forms:

1. **Panel Group Interview**: Multiple candidates are interviewed simultaneously by one or more interviewers.
2. **Group Activity Interview**: Candidates participate in team exercises or problem-solving activities while being observed.

Companies use group interviews to:

- Assess how candidates interact with others
- Observe leadership and teamwork skills in action
- Evaluate how individuals perform under pressure
- Efficiently screen multiple candidates

Preparing for a Group Interview

1. Research the Company and Role

- Understand the company's values, culture, and recent developments
- Know the job description inside out
- Prepare examples that demonstrate your relevant skills

2. Practice Group Scenarios

- Participate in mock group interviews with friends or a career coach
- Practice public speaking to boost your confidence
- Prepare answers to common interview questions

3. Develop Your Personal Brand

- Identify your unique selling points
- Prepare a concise personal pitch
- Think of specific examples that highlight your strengths

Strategies for Success in Group Interviews

1. Make a Strong First Impression

- Arrive early and introduce yourself to other candidates
- Maintain positive body language: smile, make eye contact, and offer a firm handshake
- Remember names and use them throughout the interview

2. Find the Balance Between Assertiveness and Respect

- Contribute actively without dominating the conversation
- Listen attentively to others and build on their ideas
- Avoid interrupting, but find appropriate moments to speak up

3. Showcase Your Teamwork Skills

- Encourage quieter members of the group to contribute
- Acknowledge and praise good ideas from others
- Demonstrate your ability to collaborate and find consensus

4. Demonstrate Leadership Without Overpowering

- Take initiative when appropriate, such as suggesting how to approach a group task
- Guide the conversation if it goes off-track, but do so diplomatically
- Offer to take on roles like timekeeper or note-taker in group activities

5. Use Active Listening Techniques

- Make eye contact with the person speaking
- Nod and use facial expressions to show engagement
- Summarize or paraphrase others' points to show understanding

6. Leverage Your Unique Perspective

- Bring up relevant experiences or knowledge that others might not have
- Offer a different angle on a problem or question
- Use your background to provide unique insights

7. Stay Calm Under Pressure

- Take a deep breath if you feel nervous
- If you need a moment to think, it's okay to say, "That's a great question. Let me think about that for a second."
- Maintain composure even if other candidates become competitive or aggressive

8. Be Authentic

- Don't try to be someone you're not – authenticity is key
- Share genuine opinions and ideas, even if they differ from others
- Let your personality shine through in a professional manner

Navigating Group Activities

Many group interviews include team exercises or problem-solving activities. Here's how to excel:

1. Understand the Task

- Listen carefully to instructions
- Ask clarifying questions if needed
- Suggest defining goals and roles if not explicitly stated

2. Contribute to Planning

- Propose a strategy for tackling the task
- Suggest breaking complex tasks into smaller steps
- Keep track of time and remind the group of deadlines

3. Play to Your Strengths

- Volunteer for roles that align with your skills
- Offer to take on tasks that others might be hesitant about
- Demonstrate your problem-solving skills by suggesting creative solutions

4. Foster Team Spirit

- Encourage and support your team members
- Mediate any conflicts that arise diplomatically
- Celebrate small wins and team progress

5. Focus on the Process, Not Just the Outcome

- Remember that how you work together is often more important than the final result
- Demonstrate your ability to adapt and collaborate, even if things don't go perfectly

Answering Questions in a Group Setting

When it's your turn to answer questions:

1. Be Concise but Thorough

- Get to the point quickly to respect others' time
- Use the STAR method (Situation, Task, Action, Result) for behavioral questions
- Provide specific examples to back up your points

2. Differentiate Yourself

- Highlight unique experiences or skills that set you apart
- Relate your answers to the company's needs and values
- Don't be afraid to respectfully disagree if you have a different perspective

3. Build on Others' Answers

- Reference good points made by other candidates
- Add new information or a different perspective to what's already been said
- Show that you're actively listening and engaging with the group discussion

Common Group Interview Mistakes to Avoid

1. Ignoring other candidates – remember, how you interact with peers is being evaluated
2. Dominating the conversation or interrupting others
3. Being too passive or not contributing enough
4. Displaying negative body language (eye-rolling, sighing, looking bored)
5. Arguing with or putting down other candidates
6. Failing to listen actively when others are speaking
7. Not following instructions carefully in group activities

After the Group Interview

1. Send Individual Thank-You Notes

- Email each interviewer individually within 24 hours
- Reference specific points from the interview to personalize your message
- Reiterate your interest in the position and company

2. Reflect on Your Performance

- Consider what went well and areas for improvement
- Think about how you can apply these lessons to future interviews

3. Follow Up Appropriately

- If you promised any additional information during the interview, provide it promptly
- Be patient – group interviews often take longer to process than individual interviews

Conclusion

Group interviews can be challenging, but they also offer unique opportunities to showcase your interpersonal skills, leadership potential, and ability to work in a team. By preparing thoroughly, actively participating while respecting others, and demonstrating your unique value, you can stand out positively in a group setting.

Remember, the key is to find the balance between assertiveness and collegiality. Show that you can be a strong individual contributor while also being a supportive team player. Your goal is not to "beat" the other candidates, but to demonstrate that you would be a valuable addition to the company's team.

As you practice these strategies, you'll become more comfortable with the group interview format, allowing your true skills and personality to shine through. Embrace the unique aspects of group interviews, such as the opportunity to demonstrate leadership and collaboration in real-time.

With these tools and strategies at your disposal, you're well-equipped to navigate your next group interview successfully and take the next step in your career journey. Remember, in a group interview, how you interact with others is just as important as what you say. Good luck!

Chapter 15: Negotiation Techniques: Salary and Benefits

Negotiating your salary and benefits is a crucial step in the job acceptance process. It can significantly impact your financial well-being and job satisfaction. Many job seekers find this process intimidating, but with the right techniques and preparation, you can confidently advocate for your worth. This chapter will guide you through effective negotiation strategies to help you secure a compensation package that reflects your value.

Understanding the Importance of Negotiation

1. **Financial Impact**: Even a small increase in salary can compound significantly over time.
2. **Setting Precedent**: Your starting salary often sets the base for future raises and promotions.
3. **Demonstrating Value**: Negotiation shows that you understand your worth and are committed to your career.
4. **Comprehensive Package**: Salary is just one part; benefits, perks, and work conditions are also negotiable.

Preparing for Negotiation

1. Research

- **Industry Standards**: Use websites like Glassdoor, PayScale, or industry-specific resources to understand typical salary ranges for your role and location.
- **Company Research**: Investigate the company's financial health and typical compensation practices.
- **Cost of Living**: Consider how your location affects salary expectations.

2. Know Your Worth

- **Skills Assessment**: List your unique skills, experiences, and achievements.
- **Quantify Achievements**: Prepare specific examples of how you've added value in previous roles.
- **Continuing Education**: Include any relevant certifications or advanced degrees.

3. Determine Your Targets

- **Ideal Number**: Decide on your ideal salary based on your research and personal needs.
- **Minimum Acceptable Offer**: Determine the lowest offer you'd be willing to accept.
- **Total Compensation**: Consider the entire package, including benefits, bonuses, and equity.

4. Practice

- **Role-play**: Practice negotiation scenarios with a friend or mentor.
- **Prepare Responses**: Anticipate potential objections and practice your responses.

Effective Negotiation Techniques

1. Timing is Key

- **Wait for the Right Moment**: Ideally, negotiate after you've received a formal offer but before you've accepted it.
- **Express Enthusiasm**: Always convey your excitement about the role and company.

2. Start with a Range

- **Anchoring**: Begin with a salary range slightly above your target. This gives room for negotiation while setting a higher anchor point.
- Example: "Based on my research and experience, I'm looking for a salary in the range of $X to $Y."

3. Use Silence Effectively

- After stating your request, resist the urge to fill silence. Let the other party respond first.
- This technique can often lead to a better offer as the employer fills the silence.

4. Focus on Value

- Emphasize the value you bring to the company, not your personal needs.
- Use specific examples of how your skills and experience will benefit the organization.

5. Be Collaborative, Not Adversarial

- Frame the negotiation as a problem-solving discussion to find a mutually beneficial solution.
- Use "we" language: "How can we come to an agreement that works for both of us?"

6. Consider the Entire Package

- If there's limited flexibility on salary, negotiate other aspects:
- Signing bonus
- Performance bonuses
- Stock options or equity
- Additional vacation time
- Flexible working hours or remote work options
- Professional development opportunities

7. Use Competing Offers Wisely

- If you have other offers, mention them tactfully to create leverage.
- Example: "I've received another offer that's very compelling, but I'm really excited about this opportunity. Is there any flexibility in the compensation package?"

8. Be Prepared to Walk Away

- If the offer doesn't meet your minimum requirements, be prepared to decline respectfully.
- This stance can sometimes lead to an improved offer.

Handling Common Scenarios

CHAPTER 15: NEGOTIATION TECHNIQUES: SALARY AND BENEFITS

1. When Asked About Salary Expectations Early

- Try to deflect: "I'd like to learn more about the role and your expectations before discussing compensation."
- If pressed, provide a broad range based on your research.

2. When Faced with a "Final Offer"

- Ask for time to consider the offer.
- If it's below your expectations, express your enthusiasm for the role and ask if there's any flexibility.
- Consider negotiating other benefits if salary is fixed.

3. When Offered Equity

- Understand the type of equity (e.g., stock options, RSUs) and vesting schedule.
- Ask about the company's valuation and future plans (e.g., IPO, acquisition).
- Consider seeking financial advice to understand the potential value and risks.

4. When Negotiating a Raise

- Timing is crucial: Consider the company's financial cycle and your recent achievements.
- Prepare a "brag sheet" documenting your contributions and successes.
- Frame the discussion around your value to the company, not personal needs.

The Art of Compromising

- Be willing to compromise, but do so strategically.
- If you can't get the desired base salary, try negotiating for performance-based bonuses or a salary review in 6 months.
- Consider trading off between different elements of the package (e.g., lower salary for more equity).

After the Negotiation

1. Get It in Writing

- Once you've reached an agreement, ask for the final offer in writing.
- Review all details carefully before signing.

2. Express Gratitude

- Thank the employer for their time and consideration, regardless of the outcome.
- Maintain a positive, professional relationship.

3. Fulfill Your Promises

- If you've emphasized your value during negotiations, be prepared to deliver on those promises.
- Set goals aligned with the expectations you've set.

Common Negotiation Mistakes to Avoid

1. **Accepting the First Offer**: Always negotiate, even if the initial offer seems generous.
2. **Focusing Solely on Salary**: Remember to consider the entire compensation package.

3. **Oversharing Personal Information**: Avoid basing your negotiation on personal financial needs.
4. **Being Unprepared**: Do your research and practice beforehand.
5. **Making Ultimatums**: Unless you're truly prepared to walk away, avoid ultimatums.
6. **Neglecting Non-Monetary Benefits**: These can significantly impact your job satisfaction and work-life balance.

Conclusion

Negotiating your salary and benefits is a skill that can significantly impact your career trajectory and job satisfaction. By thoroughly preparing, understanding your worth, and employing effective negotiation techniques, you can approach this process with confidence.

Remember, negotiation is not about winning or losing, but about finding a mutually beneficial agreement. Your goal is to secure a compensation package that fairly reflects your value while also aligning with the company's capabilities and standards.

Approach the negotiation process as an opportunity to demonstrate your professionalism, communication skills, and value to the organization. With practice and persistence, you'll become more comfortable and skilled at negotiating, setting yourself up for long-term career success.

Lastly, keep in mind that negotiation doesn't end when you accept a job offer. Throughout your career, you'll have opportunities to renegotiate your compensation, whether during performance reviews or when taking on new responsibilities. The skills you develop now will serve you well throughout your professional journey.

Chapter 16: Following Up: The Often Overlooked Step

In the fast-paced world of job hunting, it's easy to focus solely on preparing for and performing well in interviews. However, what you do after an interview can be just as crucial to your success. Following up is an often overlooked step that can set you apart from other candidates and demonstrate your continued interest and professionalism. This chapter will explore the art of following up throughout the job search process, from post-interview etiquette to maintaining long-term professional relationships.

The Importance of Following Up

1. **Demonstrates Interest**: Shows the employer that you're genuinely excited about the opportunity.
2. **Keeps You Top of Mind**: Reminds the hiring manager of your candidacy during the decision-making process.
3. **Provides Additional Information**: Allows you to address any points you may have missed during the interview.
4. **Shows Professionalism**: Reflects well on your work ethic and attention to detail.
5. **Builds Relationships**: Helps establish a connection that can be valuable even if you don't get this particular job.

Post-Interview Follow-Up

The Thank-You Note

Sending a thank-you note is a crucial first step in the follow-up process.
Timing:

- Send within 24 hours of the interview.
- If you interviewed with multiple people, send individual notes to each.

Format:

- Email is generally acceptable and ensures prompt delivery.
- For more traditional industries, consider a handwritten note in addition to an email.

Content:

1. Express gratitude for the interviewer's time.
2. Reiterate your interest in the position and company.
3. Briefly remind them of your qualifications.
4. Reference specific points from your conversation to personalize the message.
5. Provide any additional information promised during the interview.

Example:

```
Copy
Dear [Interviewer's Name],

Thank you for taking the time to meet with me yesterday regarding
the [Position] role at [Company]. I enjoyed learning more about
[specific aspect of the job or company discussed], and I'm even
```

more excited about the opportunity to join your team.

Our conversation about [specific project or challenge mentioned] reinforced my enthusiasm for the position. As I mentioned, my experience with [relevant skill] would allow me to hit the ground running and make immediate contributions to your team.

I look forward to hearing about the next steps in the process. Please don't hesitate to contact me if you need any additional information.

Thank you again for your time and consideration.

Best regards,
[Your Name]

Following Up on Next Steps

If you haven't heard back within the timeframe specified during the interview:

1. Wait an additional 1-2 business days beyond the specified time.
2. Send a polite email inquiring about the status of your application.

Example:

Copy
Dear [Interviewer's Name],

I hope this email finds you well. I wanted to follow up on my interview for the [Position] role, which took place on [Date]. During our conversation, you mentioned that you expected to make a decision by [specified timeframe]. I'm still very excited about the opportunity and was wondering if you could provide an update on the hiring process.

If you need any additional information from me, please don't
hesitate to ask.

Thank you for your time and consideration.

Best regards,
[Your Name]

Following Up After Rejection

Even if you don't get the job, following up can leave a positive impression and potentially lead to future opportunities.

1. Respond promptly and graciously to the rejection notice.
2. Thank them for their time and the opportunity to learn about the company.
3. Express your continued interest in the company for future opportunities.
4. Ask for feedback on your interview performance (if appropriate).

Example:

```
Copy
Dear [Interviewer's Name],

Thank you for letting me know about your decision regarding the
[Position] role. While I'm disappointed that I wasn't selected, I
appreciate the opportunity to have interviewed with you and learn
more about [Company].

I was impressed by [specific aspect of the company], and I remain
very interested in your organization. If you have any feedback on
my interview or qualifications that could help me in my job
search, I would greatly appreciate it.
```

```
Thank you again for your time and consideration. I hope our paths
cross again in the future.

Best regards,
[Your Name]
```

Long-Term Follow-Up Strategies

Following up isn't just for immediately after an interview. Maintaining professional relationships can lead to opportunities down the line.

1. **Connect on LinkedIn**: Send a personalized connection request to your interviewers.
2. **Share Relevant Content**: Occasionally share articles or insights relevant to your field or the company's interests.
3. **Provide Updates**: If you achieve a significant professional milestone, consider sharing it with your contacts.
4. **Periodic Check-Ins**: Every few months, send a brief message to stay in touch and inquire about any new opportunities.
5. **Offer Value**: If you come across information or opportunities that might benefit your contact, share it with them.

Following Up on Job Applications

When you haven't heard back after submitting an application:

1. Wait about a week after the application deadline.
2. Send a polite email to the hiring manager or HR department.
3. Reiterate your interest in the position and ask about the status of your application.

Example:

CHAPTER 16: FOLLOWING UP: THE OFTEN OVERLOOKED STEP

```
Copy
Dear [Hiring Manager's Name],

I hope this email finds you well. I submitted my application for
the [Position] role at [Company] on [Date]. I'm very excited about
the opportunity to contribute to your team, particularly in
[specific aspect of the role].

I wanted to inquire about the status of my application and the
hiring timeline for this position. If you need any additional
information from me, please let me know.

Thank you for your time and consideration.

Best regards,
[Your Name]
```

Best Practices for Following Up

1. **Be Persistent, Not Pushy**: There's a fine line between showing interest and being annoying. Use your judgment.
2. **Respect Timelines**: If the employer provides a specific timeline, wait until after that date to follow up.
3. **Keep It Professional**: Maintain a formal tone in all communications, even if your interview was casual.
4. **Proofread Carefully**: Ensure all follow-up communications are error-free.
5. **Be Prepared**: When following up by phone, be ready to discuss the position if the hiring manager is available.
6. **Add Value**: Use follow-ups as an opportunity to provide additional information about your qualifications or ideas for the role.
7. **Know When to Move On**: If you don't receive a response after 2-3 follow-ups, it's usually best to focus your energy elsewhere.

Leveraging Technology for Follow-Ups

1. **Set Reminders**: Use your calendar or a job search app to set follow-up reminders.
2. **Use Email Tracking**: Tools like Boomerang or HubSpot Sales can notify you when your emails are opened.
3. **Automation with Caution**: While some aspects of follow-up can be automated, always personalize your messages.

Conclusion

Following up is a critical step in the job search process that can significantly impact your success. It demonstrates your professionalism, enthusiasm, and attention to detail – all qualities that employers value. By mastering the art of the follow-up, you not only increase your chances of landing the job you want but also build a network of professional contacts that can benefit your career in the long term.

Remember, the goal of following up is not just to secure a specific job, but to build and maintain professional relationships. Even if a particular opportunity doesn't work out, your thoughtful follow-up can leave a lasting positive impression that may lead to future opportunities.

As you continue your job search, make following up a consistent part of your routine. With practice, it will become a natural and valuable part of your professional skill set, setting you apart in a competitive job market and positioning you for long-term career success.

Chapter 17: Dealing with Rejection and Learning from Experience

Job searching can be an emotional rollercoaster, and rejection is an inevitable part of the process. While it's natural to feel disappointed when you don't get a job you wanted, how you handle rejection can significantly impact your future success. This chapter will explore strategies for dealing with rejection constructively and turning your job search experiences into valuable learning opportunities.

Understanding Rejection in the Job Search Context

Rejection in job searching is common and often not personal. It's important to remember:

1. **Competition is Fierce**: Many qualified candidates often apply for the same position.
2. **Fit is Complex**: Companies consider various factors beyond just qualifications.
3. **Timing Matters**: Sometimes, external factors influence hiring decisions.
4. **It's a Two-Way Street**: The job might not have been the best fit for you either.

The Emotional Impact of Rejection

It's normal to experience a range of emotions after a job rejection:

1. **Disappointment**: Feeling let down after investing time and hope.
2. **Self-Doubt**: Questioning your skills and qualifications.
3. **Frustration**: Especially if you've faced multiple rejections.
4. **Anxiety**: Worries about your future and financial stability.
5. **Relief**: Sometimes, if you had reservations about the role.

Strategies for Dealing with Rejection

1. Allow Yourself to Feel

- Acknowledge your emotions without judgment.
- Give yourself time to process the disappointment.

2. Maintain Perspective

- Remember that rejection is a normal part of the job search process.
- Understand that it's not a reflection of your worth as a person or professional.

3. Practice Self-Care

- Engage in activities that boost your mood and self-esteem.
- Maintain a healthy lifestyle with proper nutrition, exercise, and sleep.

4. Seek Support

- Talk to friends, family, or a mentor about your feelings.
- Consider joining job search support groups to connect with others in similar situations.

5. Reframe the Experience

- View each rejection as a step closer to the right opportunity.
- Consider what you gained from the experience (e.g., interview practice, industry insights).

6. Stay Professional

- Respond to rejection notices graciously.
- Keep doors open for future opportunities.

Example response to a rejection:

```
Copy
Dear [Hiring Manager's Name],

Thank you for informing me of your decision regarding the
[Position] role. While I'm disappointed not to be selected, I
appreciate the opportunity to have interviewed with [Company Name].

I enjoyed learning more about your organization and am impressed
by [specific aspect of the company]. If you have any feedback on
my interview or application that could help me in my job search, I
would greatly appreciate it.

Thank you again for your time and consideration. I hope our paths
cross again in the future.

Best regards,
[Your Name]
```

Learning from the Experience

Every job application and interview, regardless of the outcome, is a learning opportunity. Here's how to make the most of your experiences:

1. Conduct a Post-Mortem Analysis

After each significant job search event (application, interview, rejection), ask yourself:

- What went well?
- What could I have done better?
- Were there any surprises I should prepare for in the future?

2. Seek Feedback

- Ask interviewers or recruiters for constructive feedback.
- Be specific in your request, e.g., "Could you provide insight into areas where I could improve my interviewing skills?"

3. Identify Patterns

- If you're facing repeated rejections, look for common themes.
- Are you consistently stumbling on certain types of questions or stages of the process?

4. Refine Your Approach

Based on your analysis and feedback:

- Update your resume and cover letter.
- Improve your interview responses.
- Enhance your skills or qualifications if necessary.

5. Expand Your Network

- Connect with interviewers on LinkedIn (when appropriate).
- Attend industry events to broaden your professional circle.

6. Reassess Your Job Search Strategy

- Are you applying for the right types of roles?
- Do you need to expand or narrow your search?
- Are you effectively showcasing your skills and experience?

Turning Rejection into Opportunity

1. Use Rejection as Motivation

- Set new goals for your job search or professional development.
- Use the experience to fuel your determination to succeed.

2. Explore Alternative Paths

- Consider contract or freelance work to gain experience.
- Look into related fields where your skills might be valuable.

3. Enhance Your Skills

- Identify skill gaps highlighted during your job search.
- Take courses, earn certifications, or work on personal projects to address these gaps.

4. Volunteer or Take on Side Projects

- Gain experience and expand your network through volunteer work.
- Start a side project that demonstrates your skills and initiative.

5. Stay Informed About the Company and Industry

- Follow companies you're interested in on social media.
- Stay updated on industry trends and news.

Building Resilience for Long-Term Success

Resilience is key to navigating the ups and downs of job searching and your overall career. Here's how to build it:

1. Develop a Growth Mindset

- View challenges as opportunities for learning and growth.
- Embrace the idea that skills and abilities can be developed through effort and learning.

2. Practice Positive Self-Talk

- Challenge negative thoughts with realistic, positive alternatives.
- Use affirmations to boost your confidence.

3. Set Realistic Expectations

- Understand that finding the right job takes time.
- Break your job search into manageable goals.

4. Celebrate Small Wins

- Acknowledge every step forward, no matter how small.
- Reward yourself for efforts, not just outcomes.

5. Maintain a Balanced Life

- Don't let your job search consume you.
- Engage in hobbies and activities that bring you joy and fulfillment.

When to Seek Professional Help

If rejection is significantly impacting your mental health or self-esteem, consider:

- Career counseling for professional guidance.
- Therapy or counseling for emotional support.

Conclusion

Rejection is an inevitable part of any job search, but it doesn't have to be a roadblock to your success. By approaching rejection with the right mindset, you can transform it from a setback into a stepping stone towards your ideal career.

Remember that every successful professional has faced rejection at some point. What sets them apart is their ability to learn from these experiences, maintain a positive attitude, and persist in pursuing their goals.

As you navigate your job search, treat each rejection as an opportunity to refine your approach, enhance your skills, and clarify your career objectives. Stay resilient, keep learning, and remain open to new possibilities. With persistence and a growth mindset, you'll not only find the right job but also develop valuable skills that will serve you throughout your career.

Your journey to professional success is a marathon, not a sprint. Each rejection brings you one step closer to the right opportunity. Stay focused on your goals, be kind to yourself, and keep moving forward. Your persistence and ability to learn from every experience will ultimately lead you to a fulfilling career that aligns with your skills, values, and aspirations.

Chapter 18: Industry-Specific Interview Tips (customize based on reader's field)

While many interview principles are universal, each industry has its unique expectations and challenges. This chapter will provide tailored advice for several major industries, helping you prepare for the specific demands of your chosen field. Remember to focus on the section most relevant to your career path.

Technology and Software Development

1. Technical Skills Assessment

- Be prepared for coding challenges, both on whiteboards and computers.
- Practice explaining your code and thought process clearly.
- Familiarize yourself with common algorithms and data structures.

2. Project Discussion

- Have detailed examples of projects you've worked on, emphasizing your role and impact.
- Be ready to discuss challenges faced and how you overcame them.

3. Staying Current

- Demonstrate knowledge of current trends and emerging technologies in your field.
- Show enthusiasm for continuous learning and self-improvement.

4. Collaboration Skills

- Highlight experiences working in Agile environments or cross-functional teams.
- Discuss how you handle code reviews and feedback.

5. System Design

- For senior roles, be prepared for system design questions.
- Practice explaining complex systems using diagrams and clear, concise language.

Finance and Banking

1. Market Knowledge

- Stay updated on current market trends, major economic events, and their potential impacts.
- Be prepared to discuss how these trends might affect the company or role you're interviewing for.

2. Technical Skills

- Be ready to demonstrate proficiency in financial modeling and analysis tools.
- Prepare to discuss specific financial concepts relevant to the role (e.g., valuation methods, risk management).

3. Regulatory Awareness

- Show understanding of key regulations in your specific area of finance (e.g., Basel III for banking, Dodd-Frank for US finance).
- Discuss how regulatory changes might impact business strategies.

4. Ethical Decision Making

- Prepare examples of how you've handled ethical dilemmas in the past.
- Demonstrate understanding of the importance of compliance and integrity in finance.

5. Stress Management

- Be ready to discuss how you handle high-pressure situations and tight deadlines.
- Provide examples of how you've maintained accuracy and attention to detail under stress.

Healthcare and Medicine

1. Patient Care Philosophy

- Articulate your approach to patient care and how it aligns with the organization's values.
- Discuss experiences that demonstrate your commitment to compassionate care.

2. Interdisciplinary Collaboration

- Highlight experiences working in multidisciplinary teams.
- Discuss how you handle disagreements or conflicts with colleagues.

3. Staying Current with Medical Advances

- Demonstrate knowledge of recent developments in your field.
- Discuss how you stay updated with the latest research and best practices.

4. Ethical Considerations

- Be prepared to discuss how you handle ethical dilemmas in patient care.
- Show understanding of patient privacy regulations and practices.

5. Technology in Healthcare

- Discuss your experience with electronic health records and other healthcare technologies.
- Show openness to adopting new technologies that improve patient care.

Marketing and Advertising

1. Portfolio Presentation

- Be prepared to walk through your portfolio, explaining the strategy behind each project.
- Highlight measurable results and impact of your campaigns.

2. Digital Marketing Proficiency

- Demonstrate understanding of various digital marketing channels and analytics tools.
- Discuss how you stay updated with rapidly changing digital trends.

3. Creative Problem Solving

- Prepare examples of how you've developed innovative solutions to marketing challenges.
- Be ready for on-the-spot creative exercises or case studies.

4. Brand Strategy

- Show understanding of brand building and management principles.
- Discuss how you align marketing strategies with overall brand goals.

5. Data-Driven Decision Making

- Highlight your ability to use data to inform marketing strategies.
- Discuss specific metrics you've used to measure campaign success.

Education

1. Teaching Philosophy

- Clearly articulate your teaching philosophy and how it aligns with the institution's values.
- Provide concrete examples of how you implement this philosophy in the classroom.

2. Classroom Management

- Discuss your approach to creating a positive learning environment.
- Provide examples of how you handle challenging student behaviors.

3. Technology Integration

- Highlight your experience with educational technology and learning management systems.
- Discuss innovative ways you've incorporated technology into your teaching.

4. Differentiation and Inclusion

- Demonstrate your ability to adapt teaching methods for diverse learners.
- Discuss strategies for creating an inclusive classroom environment.

5. Assessment and Feedback

- Explain your approach to student assessment and providing constructive feedback.
- Discuss how you use assessment data to inform your teaching.

Legal

1. Case Analysis

- Be prepared for hypothetical legal scenarios to assess your analytical skills.
- Practice articulating your reasoning clearly and concisely.

2. Research Skills

- Highlight your ability to conduct thorough legal research efficiently.
- Discuss your approach to staying updated with changing laws and precedents.

3. Client Communication

- Demonstrate your ability to explain complex legal concepts in layman's terms.
- Discuss how you handle difficult client conversations.

4. Ethical Considerations

- Be prepared to discuss how you handle ethical dilemmas in legal practice.
- Show understanding of professional conduct rules and confidentiality principles.

5. Specialization Knowledge

- Demonstrate in-depth knowledge of your area of legal specialization.
- Discuss recent developments or landmark cases in your field.

Retail and Customer Service

1. Customer Interaction Scenarios

- Be prepared for role-play exercises simulating customer interactions.
- Demonstrate your ability to handle difficult customers professionally.

2. Sales Techniques

- Discuss your approach to upselling and cross-selling.
- Highlight any notable sales achievements or targets you've met.

3. Product Knowledge

- Show enthusiasm for learning about products and services.
- Discuss how you stay updated with product information and company policies.

4. Adaptability

- Highlight your ability to work in a fast-paced, changing environment.
- Discuss how you handle unexpected situations or rushes.

5. Team Collaboration

- Provide examples of how you've contributed to a positive team environment.
- Discuss how you handle conflicts with coworkers.

General Tips for All Industries

1. Company Research

- Thoroughly research the company, its values, recent news, and major projects.
- Prepare thoughtful questions that demonstrate your interest and knowledge.

2. Industry Trends

- Stay informed about major trends and challenges in your industry.
- Be prepared to discuss how these trends might impact the role you're interviewing for.

3. Soft Skills

- Regardless of industry, emphasize crucial soft skills like communication, teamwork, and problem-solving.
- Provide specific examples that demonstrate these skills in action.

4. Cultural Fit

- Research the company culture and be prepared to discuss how you would fit in.
- Ask questions about the work environment and team dynamics.

5. Continuous Learning

- Highlight your commitment to professional development and continuous learning.
- Discuss any relevant certifications, courses, or self-study you've undertaken recently.

Conclusion

While these industry-specific tips provide a strong foundation, remember that every company and role is unique. Tailor your preparation to the specific position you're applying for, using the job description as a guide. Combine these industry-specific insights with the general interview strategies discussed in earlier chapters to present yourself as a well-rounded, informed candidate.

Remember, the key to interview success lies not just in showcasing your technical skills and industry knowledge, but also in demonstrating your passion for the field, your ability to adapt and learn, and your potential to contribute meaningfully to the organization. By thoroughly preparing with these industry-specific tips and maintaining a positive, professional demeanor, you'll be well-equipped to impress in your next interview and take a significant step forward in your career journey.

Chapter 19: The Future of Interviews: AI and Automation

As technology continues to advance at a rapid pace, the landscape of job interviews is evolving. Artificial Intelligence (AI) and automation are increasingly playing significant roles in the hiring process, from initial candidate screening to final selection. This chapter will explore the current trends, future predictions, and strategies for job seekers to navigate this new terrain successfully.

Current Trends in AI and Automation in Hiring

1. AI-Powered Resume Screening

Many companies now use Applicant Tracking Systems (ATS) with AI capabilities to screen resumes. These systems can:

- Parse resumes for relevant keywords and experiences
- Rank candidates based on job requirements
- Eliminate candidates who don't meet minimum qualifications

Candidate Strategy: Optimize your resume with relevant keywords from the job description, ensuring it's ATS-friendly.

2. Chatbots for Initial Screening

AI-powered chatbots are being used to conduct initial candidate screenings. They can:

- Ask basic qualifying questions
- Provide information about the company and role
- Schedule interviews with human recruiters

Candidate Strategy: Be prepared for text-based interactions early in the application process. Respond promptly and professionally, even if you suspect you're interacting with a bot.

3. Video Interview Analysis

Some companies use AI to analyze pre-recorded video interviews. These systems can assess:

- Facial expressions and emotions
- Voice tone and speech patterns
- Word choice and language use

Candidate Strategy: Practice your video interview skills, focusing on clear speech, positive body language, and maintaining eye contact with the camera.

4. AI-Assisted Skill Assessments

Online skill assessments powered by AI are becoming more sophisticated, testing not just technical knowledge but also problem-solving abilities and soft skills.
Candidate Strategy: Familiarize yourself with online testing platforms and practice taking assessments in your field.

CHAPTER 19: THE FUTURE OF INTERVIEWS: AI AND AUTOMATION

Predictions for the Future of AI in Interviews

1. Virtual Reality (VR) Interviews

VR technology could create immersive interview experiences, allowing candidates to:

- Demonstrate skills in simulated work environments
- Interact with virtual team members
- Showcase spatial and problem-solving skills in 3D environments

Future Preparation: Stay open to new technologies and be willing to adapt to novel interview formats.

2. Advanced Emotion Recognition

Future AI might analyze microexpressions and physiological responses to assess:

- Truthfulness of responses
- Stress levels and composure
- Cultural fit and interpersonal skills

Future Preparation: Work on emotional intelligence and stress management techniques.

3. Predictive Performance Modeling

AI could use vast datasets to predict a candidate's likely job performance and career trajectory based on their background, skills, and interview responses.
   Future Preparation: Focus on continual skill development and be prepared to discuss your long-term career goals and adaptability.

4. Personalized Interview Experiences

AI might tailor the interview process to each candidate, adjusting questions and assessments based on real-time performance and responses.

Future Preparation: Be flexible and ready to engage with a wide range of questions and tasks during interviews.

Ethical Considerations and Limitations

As AI becomes more prevalent in hiring, several ethical concerns arise:

1. Bias in AI Algorithms

AI systems can inadvertently perpetuate or amplify biases present in their training data.

Candidate Awareness: Be aware of potential biases and be prepared to showcase your skills and experiences clearly, regardless of background.

2. Privacy Concerns

The collection and analysis of extensive personal data during the interview process raise privacy issues.

Candidate Strategy: Be mindful of the information you share and understand your rights regarding data collection and usage.

3. Lack of Human Touch

Over-reliance on AI could lead to a less personal hiring process, potentially missing nuanced aspects of a candidate's suitability.

Candidate Strategy: Look for opportunities to showcase your personality and soft skills, even in automated processes.

4. Accessibility Issues

Some AI-driven interview technologies might not be equally accessible to all candidates.
Candidate Awareness: If you have concerns about accessibility, don't hesitate to communicate with the hiring company about accommodations.

Strategies for Success in an AI-Driven Interview Process

1. Embrace Technology

- Stay updated with the latest interview technologies
- Practice with AI-powered interview preparation tools
- Be open to new forms of assessment and interaction

2. Focus on Both Hard and Soft Skills

- Develop a strong balance of technical skills and emotional intelligence
- Be prepared to demonstrate problem-solving abilities in various formats
- Cultivate adaptability and learning agility

3. Build a Strong Online Presence

- Maintain a professional and active LinkedIn profile
- Showcase projects and skills on relevant platforms (e.g., GitHub for developers)
- Ensure consistency across all online professional profiles

4. Understand the Company's Tech Stack

- Research the AI and automation tools commonly used in your industry
- Familiarize yourself with any publicly known hiring technologies used by target companies

5. Prepare for Data-Driven Questions

- Be ready to provide specific, quantifiable examples of your achievements
- Practice explaining your problem-solving process clearly and logically

6. Maintain Authenticity

- While adapting to AI-driven processes, don't lose your personal touch
- Find ways to convey your unique personality and values, even in automated stages

7. Seek Human Connection

- Whenever possible, try to establish a personal connection with human recruiters or hiring managers
- Use follow-up opportunities to add a personal touch to your application

The Human Element: Where AI Falls Short

Despite advancements in AI, certain human qualities remain challenging to assess automatically:

1. **Creative Problem-Solving**: The ability to think outside the box in unique situations.
2. **Emotional Intelligence**: Nuanced interpersonal skills and empathy.
3. **Cultural Fit**: The subtle aspects of how well a candidate might integrate into a team.
4. **Potential and Adaptability**: The capacity for growth and handling unforeseen challenges.

Candidate Strategy: Highlight these qualities in your interactions, especially when you have the opportunity to communicate directly with human interviewers.

Balancing AI and Human Judgment

The future of interviewing likely lies in a balanced approach, combining the efficiency of AI with the nuanced judgment of human recruiters. Companies may use AI to:

1. Streamline initial screenings
2. Provide data-driven insights to support decision-making
3. Reduce unconscious bias in the hiring process

While human recruiters focus on:

1. Assessing complex interpersonal skills
2. Making nuanced judgments about team fit
3. Selling the company and role to top candidates

Candidate Strategy: Prepare for both AI-driven assessments and human interactions, recognizing the value each brings to the hiring process.

Conclusion

The integration of AI and automation into the interview process represents both challenges and opportunities for job seekers. While these technologies can make the hiring process more efficient and potentially more objective, they also require candidates to adapt their preparation and presentation strategies.

As you navigate this evolving landscape, remember that the fundamental goal of the interview process remains the same: to find the best match between candidate and company. By staying informed about technological trends, continuously developing your skills, and maintaining your authentic human touch, you can position yourself for success in the interviews of the future.

Embrace the changes brought by AI and automation, but don't lose sight of the uniquely human qualities that make you a valuable candidate. The future of interviews may be high-tech, but the future of work will always require the creativity, adaptability, and interpersonal skills that define us as human beings. By balancing technological savvy with these timeless human qualities, you'll be well-prepared to succeed in the interviews of today and tomorrow.

Chapter 20: Your 30-Day Interview Preparation Plan

Preparing for a job interview can be a daunting task, but with a structured approach, you can significantly increase your chances of success. This 30-day plan will guide you through a comprehensive preparation process, covering all aspects of interview readiness. Remember to adjust the plan as needed based on your specific circumstances and the time you have available.

Week 1: Laying the Groundwork

Day 1-2: Self-Assessment and Goal Setting

- Reflect on your career goals and aspirations
- Review your skills, strengths, and areas for improvement
- Set clear objectives for your job search

Day 3-4: Resume and LinkedIn Profile Update

- Update your resume with recent achievements and experiences
- Tailor your resume to the job descriptions you're targeting
- Refresh your LinkedIn profile, ensuring consistency with your resume

Day 5: Job Market Research

- Research companies in your industry of interest
- Identify potential job openings that match your skills and goals
- Create a list of target companies and positions

Day 6-7: Networking Preparation

- Update your elevator pitch
- Reach out to contacts in your target companies or industries
- Join relevant professional groups on LinkedIn or other platforms

Week 2: Skill Development and Interview Basics

Day 8-9: Technical Skill Refresher

- Review key technical skills required for your target roles
- Complete online tutorials or courses to brush up on important areas

Day 10-11: Soft Skill Enhancement

- Practice active listening and clear communication
- Work on your body language and non-verbal communication skills
- Develop strategies for managing interview stress

Day 12-13: Common Interview Questions

- Research and prepare answers for common interview questions
- Practice the STAR method for behavioral questions
- Prepare your "Tell me about yourself" response

Day 14: Mock Interview - Round 1

- Conduct a mock interview with a friend or mentor
- Record the session if possible for later review
- Gather feedback on your responses and overall presentation

Week 3: Deep Dive and Customization

Day 15-16: Company Research

- Conduct in-depth research on your target companies
- Understand their products/services, culture, and recent news
- Prepare questions to ask the interviewer based on your research

Day 17-18: Industry Trends and Challenges

- Study current trends and challenges in your industry
- Prepare to discuss how these trends might impact the role you're applying for

Day 19-20: Salary Research and Negotiation Prep

- Research salary ranges for your target positions and locations
- Develop a negotiation strategy
- Practice discussing salary expectations

Day 21: Personal Branding

- Refine your personal brand statement
- Ensure your online presence aligns with your professional brand
- Prepare examples that demonstrate your unique value proposition

Week 4: Fine-tuning and Final Preparations

Day 22-23: Behavioral Interview Preparation

- Develop a bank of stories that showcase your skills and experiences
- Practice adapting these stories to different types of behavioral questions
- Focus on quantifiable achievements and results

Day 24: Technical Interview Practice

- If applicable, practice technical problems or case studies
- Review key concepts relevant to your field
- Prepare to explain your problem-solving process

Day 25: Mock Interview - Round 2

- Conduct another mock interview, focusing on areas for improvement identified in the first round
- Practice with someone unfamiliar if possible to simulate a real interview experience

Day 26: Interview Logistics

- Plan your interview outfit
- Prepare your interview portfolio or any materials you need to bring
- Research the interview location and plan your route

Day 27: Final Resume and Application Review

- Give your resume and application materials a final review
- Ensure all information is up-to-date and error-free
- Prepare additional copies of your resume to bring to interviews

CHAPTER 20: YOUR 30-DAY INTERVIEW PREPARATION PLAN

Day 28: Mental Preparation and Self-Care

- Practice relaxation techniques to manage interview anxiety
- Review your achievements and remind yourself of your value
- Get a good night's sleep

Day 29: Day-Before Preparation

- Review key points about the company and role
- Prepare questions for the interviewer
- Do a final check of your interview outfit and materials
- Avoid last-minute cramming; focus on relaxation and confidence-building

Day 30: Interview Day

- Wake up early and eat a healthy breakfast
- Review your prepared materials one last time
- Arrive at the interview location early
- Take deep breaths and use positive self-talk to calm nerves

Additional Tips for Success

1. **Consistency is Key**: Stick to your preparation plan as much as possible. Regular, consistent preparation is more effective than last-minute cramming.
2. **Flexibility**: Be prepared to adjust your plan if you secure an interview earlier than expected. Prioritize company-specific research when you have a concrete interview scheduled.
3. **Continuous Learning**: Use this month to also expand your knowledge of your field. Read industry publications, attend webinars, or participate in relevant online forums.
4. **Network Throughout**: Don't wait until the end of your preparation to

start networking. Engage with your professional network throughout the month.
5. **Practice Active Reflection**: After each preparation activity, take a few minutes to reflect on what you've learned and how you can apply it in an interview setting.
6. **Tailor Your Approach**: While this plan provides a general structure, make sure to tailor your preparation to your specific industry and the types of roles you're pursuing.
7. **Balance**: While thorough preparation is important, avoid over-preparing to the point of stress or burnout. Maintain a balance with other aspects of your life.
8. **Positive Mindset**: Throughout your preparation, maintain a positive, growth-oriented mindset. View each step as an opportunity to improve and showcase your best self.

Conclusion

This 30-day plan provides a comprehensive approach to interview preparation, covering everything from self-assessment and skill development to final-day preparations. By following this structured plan and putting in consistent effort, you'll build both the skills and the confidence needed to excel in your interviews.

Remember, the goal of this preparation isn't just to secure a job offer, but to find a role that aligns with your skills, values, and career aspirations. Use this preparation time to not only improve your interview performance but also to gain clarity on your professional goals and the type of organization where you'll thrive.

As you work through this plan, be kind to yourself and celebrate your progress along the way. Interview preparation is a journey of professional and personal growth. Regardless of the immediate outcome of any single interview, the skills and self-awareness you develop during this process will serve you well throughout your career.

Approach your interviews with confidence, knowing that you've put in

CHAPTER 20: YOUR 30-DAY INTERVIEW PREPARATION PLAN

the work to prepare thoroughly. Good luck!

Conclusion: Mastering the Art of Job Interviews

As we conclude this comprehensive guide to job interview success, it's important to reflect on the journey we've taken together. From understanding the modern interview landscape to crafting your personal brand, from mastering body language to navigating the complexities of AI-driven hiring processes, we've covered a wide range of strategies and techniques to help you excel in your job search.

Key Takeaways

Let's revisit some of the most crucial points from each chapter:

1. **The Modern Job Interview Landscape**: We explored how interviews have evolved, emphasizing the importance of adaptability in facing various interview formats and technologies.
2. **Mastering Your Mindset**: We discussed the critical role of confidence and positivity in interview success, providing strategies to cultivate a winning attitude.
3. **Research Techniques**: We emphasized the importance of thorough company and industry research, showing how this knowledge can set you apart from other candidates.
4. **Crafting Your Personal Brand**: We guided you through the process of developing a unique professional identity that resonates with potential

employers.
5. **Resume Optimization for ATS**: We provided strategies to ensure your resume passes through Applicant Tracking Systems while still appealing to human readers.
6. **The Art of the Elevator Pitch**: We helped you craft a concise, compelling summary of your professional value.
7. **Body Language Secrets**: We explored the power of nonverbal communication and how to use it to your advantage in interviews.
8. **Answering Common Questions with the STAR Method**: We introduced a structured approach to answering behavioral questions effectively.
9. **Tackling Behavioral Questions**: We delved deeper into strategies for excelling in behavioral interviews.
10. **Navigating Tricky Situational Questions**: We provided techniques for handling complex, hypothetical scenarios.
11. **Showcasing Your Soft Skills**: We discussed how to effectively demonstrate crucial interpersonal skills during the interview process.
12. **Technical Interview Strategies**: We offered field-specific advice for excelling in technical interviews across various industries.
13. **Remote Interview Success**: We explored the nuances of virtual interviews and how to master this increasingly common format.
14. **Group Interview Dynamics**: We provided strategies for standing out positively in group interview settings.
15. **Negotiation Techniques**: We guided you through the process of negotiating salary and benefits effectively.
16. **Following Up**: We emphasized the importance of post-interview communication and how to do it effectively.
17. **Dealing with Rejection**: We provided strategies for handling rejection constructively and learning from each interview experience.
18. **Industry-Specific Tips**: We offered tailored advice for interviews in various fields, recognizing the unique demands of different industries.
19. **The Future of Interviews**: We explored the growing role of AI and automation in the hiring process and how to prepare for these changes.

20. **30-Day Interview Preparation Plan**: We concluded with a structured plan to help you prepare comprehensively for your interviews.

The Holistic Approach to Interview Success

As you reflect on these chapters, remember that interview success is not about mastering a single skill or technique. It's about adopting a holistic approach that combines thorough preparation, self-awareness, adaptability, and authentic self-presentation.

1. **Preparation is Key**: Across all chapters, we've emphasized the importance of thorough preparation. Whether it's researching the company, practicing your responses, or understanding industry trends, preparation gives you the confidence to handle whatever comes your way in an interview.
2. **Authenticity Matters**: While we've provided numerous strategies and techniques, it's crucial to remain authentic. The best interviews feel like genuine conversations, not rehearsed performances. Use the tools we've provided to present the best version of your authentic self.
3. **Continuous Learning**: The job market and interview processes are constantly evolving. Commit to continuous learning and improvement, staying updated with industry trends and refining your interview skills throughout your career.
4. **Resilience and Positivity**: Job searching can be challenging, but maintaining a positive attitude and learning from each experience is crucial. Remember, every interview, regardless of the outcome, is an opportunity for growth.
5. **Tailoring Your Approach**: While we've provided general strategies, always tailor your approach to the specific company, role, and industry. What works in one interview may not be appropriate for another.

Beyond the Interview: Long-Term Career Success

While this book has focused on mastering the job interview process, many of the skills and strategies we've discussed are valuable throughout your career:

1. **Communication Skills**: The ability to articulate your thoughts clearly and persuasively is crucial in any professional role.
2. **Self-Awareness**: Understanding your strengths, weaknesses, and values will guide you in making the right career decisions.
3. **Research and Preparation**: The habit of thorough preparation will serve you well in all aspects of your professional life.
4. **Adaptability**: As we've seen with the rise of remote interviews and AI in hiring, the ability to adapt to change is invaluable in today's fast-paced work environment.
5. **Networking**: The networking skills you develop during your job search will continue to be important for career growth and professional development.
6. **Negotiation**: The ability to negotiate effectively is crucial not just for job offers, but for navigating various workplace situations.
7. **Continuous Improvement**: The mindset of learning from experiences and constantly seeking to improve will drive your long-term career success.

Final Thoughts

As you embark on your job search journey, remember that landing the right job is not just about impressing the interviewer—it's about finding a role and an organization that aligns with your skills, values, and career aspirations. Use the interview process as an opportunity not just to showcase your abilities, but also to evaluate whether the position and company are the right fit for you.

Approach each interview as a learning experience. Even if you don't get the job, you'll gain valuable insights about yourself, refine your interview skills, and potentially open doors to other opportunities.

Remember, too, that your worth is not defined by any single interview or job. Stay confident in your abilities and persistent in your efforts. The right opportunity will come along, and with the strategies and mindset you've developed through this book, you'll be well-prepared to seize it.

As you move forward, stay curious, remain open to new experiences, and never stop investing in your professional development. The job market will continue to evolve, and so should you. Embrace each challenge as an opportunity for growth, and approach your career with enthusiasm and determination.

Thank you for joining me on this journey through the intricacies of job interviewing. I hope the insights and strategies in this book serve you well in your current job search and throughout your career. Remember, you have unique talents and experiences to offer. Go forth with confidence, showcase your authentic self, and make your mark in the professional world.

Best of luck in your interviews and your future career endeavors. You've got this!

Chapter 23

www.ingramcontent.com/pod-product-compliance
Lightning Source LLC
Chambersburg PA
CBHW071830210526
45479CB00001B/74